C000152696

Landscapes of
SLOVENIA

a countryside guide
Second edition

David Robertson
and
Sarah Stewart

SUNFLOWER BOOKS

Second edition © 2005
Sunflower Books™
PO Box 36160
London SW7 3WS, UK
www.sunflowerbooks.co.uk

Published in the USA by
Hunter Publishing Inc
130 Campus Drive
Edison, NJ 08818
www.hunterpublishing.com

All rights reserved.
No part of this publication may
be reproduced, stored in a
retrieval system, or transmitted
by any form or by any means,
electronic, mechanical,
photocopying, recording
or otherwise, without the
prior written permission
of the publishers.

ISBN 1-85691-285-X

Signpost at Velika Planina (Walk 36)

Important note to the reader

We have tried to ensure that the descriptions and maps in this book are error-free at press date. The book will be updated, where necessary, whenever future printings permit. It will be very helpful for us to receive your comments (sent in care of the publishers, please) for the updating of future printings.

We also rely on those who use this book — especially walkers — to take along a good supply of common sense when they explore. Conditions can change fairly rapidly in Slovenia, and *storm damage, tree-felling, earthquakes, bulldozing or snow and ice may make a route unsafe at any time*. If the route is not as we outline it here, and your way ahead is not secure, return to the point of departure. *Never attempt to complete a tour or walk under hazardous conditions!* Please read carefully the notes on pages 37-43, as well as the introductory comments at the beginning of each tour and walk (regarding road conditions, equipment, grade, distances and time, etc). Explore *safely*, while at the same time respecting the beauty of the countryside.

Cover photograph: Slap Mostnice (Walk 22)
Title page: window at Srednja Vas (Car tour 1, Walk 23)

Photographs: David Robertson
Maps: John Underwood
A CIP catalogue record for this book is available from the British Library.
Printed and bound in England: J H Haynes & Co Ltd

10 9 8 7 6 5 4 3 2 1

Contents

4   Landscapes of Slovenia

Touring map/transport information   *inside back cover*

☀ Preface

Slovenia borders Italy, Austria, Hungary and Croatia and was once part of the Austro-Hungarian Empire. In 1918, after the First World War, Slovenia was amalgamated into Yugoslavia before finally gaining independence in 1991. Happily it has avoided all the recent troubles of the neighbouring Balkan states and today is a modern country, western in outlook. In May 2004 Slovenia joined the European Union.

The people are prosperous, friendly and eager to share their pride in the beauty and heritage of their homeland. Tourist facilities are modern, spotlessly clean and blend in sensitively with the countryside.

'Small is beautiful', a much-used cliché, certainly applies to Slovenia, which is only half the size of Switzerland. With a population of only two million, the landscape is still essentially rural. The jagged snow-capped peaks of the Julian Alps contrast with fertile valleys, full of colour and activity. The porous limestone rock has created the Karst landscape. Typical features can be seen everywhere and are exciting to explore. Underground rivers appear from rock faces and cascade down in dramatic waterfalls, narrow gorges are carved through the cliffs, while caves and natural rock arches abound.

Slovenians love the land and, while only about 10 per cent farm full time, more than 25 per cent of the population grow some of their own food. Farming is mainly traditional. The mountain valleys are immaculate, with strips of vegetables and corn amidst the hayfields and orchards. There are hop-growing areas and beautiful vineyards. Amongst these industrious people one senses an orderly contentment and a feeling that everything is in tune with nature.

All over the country there are opportunities for walking and exploring and, in this book, we would like to share with you our love of Slovenia. You will climb exhilarating mountains, discover both well-known and more hidden natural phenomena and wander through enchanting villages.

— David Robertson and Sarah Stewart

View from Luknja to the cliffs of Kanjavec (Walk 7)

Replica beehive panels at Dovje (detour on Car tour 1); see also box on page 48.

Acknowledgements

We are most grateful to the tourist information centres that we visited, Danilo Miklavže Sbrizaj of the Alpine Association of Slovenia, Eva Štravs of Tourism Bled and Miram Hladnik, all of whom gave us valuable assistance. We would also like to thank particularly Lydia Koren of Kamp Koren, Kobarid and Nika Moric of Camping Bled for all their help and kindness, and the many Slovenians who made us so welcome in their country. Friends and family have been full of enthusiasm and encouragement, and a special thanks to Damaris Fletcher for her constructive editing. For advice on scanning and digital imaging we would like to thank John Seccombe of Sunflower Books. For the hard work involved in drawing the maps our thanks to John Underwood. We are sincerely grateful to our publisher, Pat Underwood, who has given us the opportunity and confidence to write this guide.

Getting there and getting about

Flying to Brnik, Ljubljana, the only international airport with flights from the UK and Ireland, is the best option for a short visit. Adria Airways, Slovenia's national airline (www. adria-airways.com) flies from London Gatwick, Manchester and Dublin; Easyjet flies from London Stansted. It is easy to rent a car from firms like Budget, Avis and Hertz, which all have offices in large towns and at the airport, and there are also independent rental agencies. Package tours are on offer too — the usual centres being Bled, the Bohinj Valley, Kranska Gora and the coastal resorts.

It is quite feasible to **take your own car** from Britain if you are planning a longer stay. The journey from the Channel ports to Slovenia can be driven in less than two days. The motorways through Belgium and Germany are toll-free, but to drive through Austria you must purchase a 'vignette' (available at or before the border from petrol stations). The drive is easy and picturesque.

Undoubtedly the best way to enjoy Slovenia and reach all the walks in this book easily is with a car, but we have also tried to cater for those visitors who do not have their own transport. The provincial **bus service** is both reliable and reasonable, and all towns in Slovenia are linked by the bus network. Some walks start from town centres, but for those in remoter locations we have always indicated if buses stop nearby. The tourist information centres will provide you with up-to-date timetables to supplement the information given on the touring map. **Taxis** are only available in some towns.

For those visitors based in Ljubljana, **trains** and buses radiate out to all regions. Walks around Bled and Bohinj are easily accessible as a day out from the capital.

Coach tours are less than ideal for walking, but do give an introduction to this beautiful country. Many start from Bled or Ljubljana and go to some of the areas and attractions we visit on our walks.

Cycling is a wonderful way to explore Slovenia. By camping and staying in hostels or B&Bs, nearly all our walks are easily accessible. Bikes can be carried on trains and, if there is room, on buses. Contact the Cyclists Touring Club or Slovenian Tourist Board for further information (see page 41).

❃ Picnicking

Outdoor eating is an important part of any holiday and in Slovenia there are many wonderful, easily-reached picnic spots. We have indicated on the touring map the more attractive roadside picnic areas, but we would suggest that you park your car and venture away from the road.

Below are our favourite picnic places. Some are just off the road, while to reach others requires a bit more effort that will be rewarded by seclusion and views. All are easily accessible, some following one of the walks described in the book for a short distance, others making excellent short walks in themselves.

The symbol *P* printed in green on the appropriate walking or touring map indicates the location of the picnic, and many of them are illustrated. The symbol ○ indicates a picnic in full sun. **All picnickers should read the Country code on page 40 and go quietly in the countryside**.

Enjoy the country's many delicious breads and the wide variety of cheeses, smoked meats and fruit, washed down by the inexpensive local beer or wine, fruit juice or bottled water.

1 Lake Bled: north shore *(map page 44 or 47, photograph page 44)*

🚗 (Car tour 1) Park in Bled. 5-25min on foot. Picnic in the park or further along the shore on the lakeside benches. *Not our most secluded spot, but who can resist a picnic enjoying the tranquil views of the castle, Otok and the church.*

2 Lake Bled: Osojnica viewpoint or south shore *(map page 44 or 47, photographs pages 16, 45)*

🚗 (Car tour 1) From Bled drive through Mlino and then turn right after the Bled Hotel to return to the lakeside. Park near the entrance to the campsite. There are then two possibilities.
a) 35min on foot. Wear stout shoes. Follow Walk 1 on page 44 from the 37min-point to the upper Osojnica viewpoint. *From here you enjoy picture-postcard views across*

8

Lake Bled to the mountains beyond (photograph page 45).
b) 12min on foot. Follow (a), but omit the climb to the viewpoint; continue around the lake to our 'Lovers' seat'. *A fairytale scene and the 'classic' view of Otok and Bled Castle shown on page 16.*

3 Triglav face to face *(map page 58, photographs opposite)*

🚗 (Car tour 1) Follow the driving directions for Walk 7, stopping on the way to visit the picturesque waterfalls of Peričnik (visited on Alternative Walk 7 and shown on page 59). 15min on foot. Follow Walk 7 to just beyond the 'piton' memorial, where there is a pleasant grassy area. *Enjoy the awe-inspiring grandeur of Slovenia's highest mountain, Triglav, from near the foot of its towering north face.*

Top: view to Triglav and V. Draški Vrh from Viševnik (Walk 6); above: the summit of Triglav from V. Draški Vrh (Alternative walk 6); right: the 'piton' memorial to the Partisan mountaineers in the Vrata Valley (Picnic 3, Walk 7)

Triglav — 'Old Three Heads'

The only national park in Slovenia is called after its highest and most famous mountain, Triglav. This centrepiece of the Julian Alps, at 2864m (9394ft), has three beautiful peaks. In folklore it was considered a three-headed god keeping a watchful eye on the earth, sky and the underworld. The summit was first reached in 1778, and the mountain features on the country's national flag.

It is expected that all true Slovenians should climb to the summit at least once in their lives, and many do so every year. The ascent involves a minimum of one overnight stay in a mountain hut and is, therefore, beyond the scope of this book. For any intrepid mountaineers there is plenty of information available on routes, and guides can be hired from local tourist agencies and the Alpine Association (PZS; see page 38).

9

4 Vršič (map page 66) ○

🚗 (Car tour 1) Park at the top of the Vršič Pass (paid parking). 🚐 from Kranjska Gora or Bovec. Approximately 30min on foot. Walk up the gravel track beside the Tičarjev Dom and follow signs to Poštarski Dom. Picnic on one of the nearby grassy hills. *Enjoy stunning mountain scenery opposite the amazing Ajdovska Deklica (Girl's Face), on the cliffs of Prisank.*

5 Kugy Monument
(map page 69)

🚗 (Car tour 1) Park off the road at Bend No. 48 on the south side of the Vršič Pass. 🚐 Buses stop nearby. 2min on foot. Follow the signposted footpath (Walk 12) to the statue, and picnic nearby. *Wonderful views of the Trenta Valley and of Jalovec (2645m), one of Slovenia's most difficult mountains to climb.*

River Soča — Velika Korita (Car tour 1, Picnic 6)

6 River Soča *(see the touring map, photograph opposite)*

🚗 (Car tour 1) 2.5km/1.5mi south of the church in Soča, take the turn signposted for Lepena and park by the footbridge 500m down the road. 5min on foot. Picnic on the gravel beach or on the flat rocks a little higher upstream at the entrance to the Velika Korita. *Enjoy the blue, blue Soča River and this amazing ravine (see Car tour 1 for details).*

7 Tolmin Gorges *(map page 84, nearby photograph page 85)*

🚗 (Car tour 1) From the centre of Tolmin, turn north beside the post office (Posta) towards Zatolmin and then turn right for 'Tolminska'. Park just beyond the bar. 5min on foot. Walk up the road for one minute and then turn right down a path that leads to the river and picnic beside it. *This lovely riverside picnic spot is at the hub of Walk 18, and all the main highlights are only a few minutes away.*

8 Most na Soči *(see the touring map)*

🚗 (Car Tours 1 and 2) Park beside the river Soča just north of Most na Soči on the road to Tolmin. 5-15min on foot. Follow the riverside path to your chosen spot. *The river is dammed here to form a small lake, and its colour is truly amazing. This is a peaceful spot away from the busy road.*

9 Bohinjsko Jezero *(map pages 90-91, photograph pages 88-89)*

🚗 (Car tour 1) and 🚌. For access details, see Walk 20, page 88. Minimum of 5-15min on foot. Follow Walk 20 for as long as you like. *Ideal picnicking on the shores of the lake — take a swimsuit.*

10 Mostnica Gorge *(map page 94, photograph page 92)*

🚗 (Car tour 1) and 🚌. For access details, see Walk 22, page 93. 20-30min on foot. Follow Walk 22 to the 'Toblerone'-shaped hut and then walk either side of the gorge. Keep left to reach a grassy area or keep right to reach some flat rocks. *Enjoy the amazing rock formations and deep pools of this rushing river.*

11 Peč viewpoint *(map page 95)*

🚗 (Car tour 1) and 🚌. For access details, see Walk 23, page 95. 30min on foot. Follow Walk 23 and take the detour to Peč. *Picnic while enjoying a classic view of the church and bridge at Ribčev Laz and Bohinjsko Jezero. This is a rocky picnic spot.*

12 Vogel ski area *(map page 99)*

🚗 (Car tour 1) and 🚌. For access details, see Walk 24, page 98. Minimum of 5min on foot. Walk as little or as far as you like around the ski centre. *A picnic with spectacular views over Bohinjsko Jezero and to Triglav.*

13 Predmeja *(map page 102)*

🚗 (Car tour 2) See Walk 27, page 102. This is a roadside picnic area about 500m east of the starting point for Walk 27. *A very scenic area with tremendous views south across the Vipava Valley. Several well-signposted short walks start from here.*

14 Stari Grad, Vipava *(see the touring map)*

🚗 (Car tour 2) After turning left for Vipava, park in the large car park on your left. From here the castle of Stari Grad is clearly visible. 21min on foot. Walk to the village, crossing the bridge on Beblerjeva Ulica and then pass a large white church. At the far end of Trg Pavla Rušpa turn right and then immediately left up a street (where 'Nanos' is painted on a cornerstone). From here target marks (see opposite) can be followed. Turn left at No.7 Gradrijanova Ulica and continue up the narrow road to the right of a shrine. At the end of the asphalt road turn right by No. 40 Na Hribu and climb a narrow path into the trees. At a T-junction turn left to find the ruined castle. Picnic on the rocky promontory on the far side of the ruins, which unfortunately are too unstable for exploration. *Superb views over this famous 'wine' valley.*

15 Hrastovlje *(map page 106, photographs pages 26 and 105)*

🚗 (Car tour 3) For access details, see Walk 28, page 104. 5min on foot. Walk up to the church and go round it to the left. Picnic just beyond the church on a quiet grassy bank. *Lovely views of the valley and along the amazing limestone escarpment.*

16 By the Škocjan Caves *(map page 107, photograph page 25)*

🚗 (Car tour 3) For access details, see Walk 29, page 107. 12-18min on foot. Follow Walk 29 past the viewpoint (6min; the photograph on page 25 was taken here) and then turn right. a) Picnic in one of several clear areas beside the path overlooking the steep cliffs. b) Four minutes further on there is a small field on the left. c) Continue on the path and, where it divides, go straight up to the brow of the hill. Turn sharp right for a pleasant spot looking over to Škocjan church and down into one of the collapsed caves. *Picnic in this amazing landscape of cliffs and collapsed caves and perhaps explore further by following Short walk 29-1 or 29-2. Note: only picnic suggestion (b) is suitable for small children.*

17 Rakov Škocjan *(map page 111)*

Car (Car tour 4) For access details, see Walk 31, page 111 (you can also park beside the hotel). 5-30min on foot. There are plenty of picnic opportunities in this enchanting place. Just follow Walk 31 until you find your ideal spot. *One of our favourites is beside the river just after Board 9.*

18 Snežnik Castle *(see the touring map, photographs pages 29, 110)*

🚗 (Car tour 4) Park in the castle car park. 5-10min on foot. *Snežnik is a beautiful moated castle in extensive parkland.*

19 Slivniško Jezero *(see the touring map, photograph page 32)* ○

🚗 (Car tour 5) Follow directions from Gorica (the 72km-point, page 31). 5-15min on foot. Walk as far as you like along the grassy banks of this reservoir. *A peaceful spot with views across the water.*

20 Rogla *(map page 119, photograph opposite)*

🚗 (Car tour 5) For access details, see Walk 34, page 118. 15-20min on foot. Follow Walk 34 to a grassy area with extensive views over the forested plateau. *A gentle stroll in the clear mountain air.*

21 Ptuj *(see the touring map, photograph pages 30-31)* ○

🚗 (Car tour 5) Park in the car park on the west side of the river Drava. 5-10min on foot. Walk towards the town and turn left along the river bank just before the footbridge. *The grassy banks beside the wide, slow-moving river Drava provide a peaceful setting with perfect views of Ptuj.*

Top: the wide open spaces near Rogla on the Pohorje Massif (Picnic 20, Walk 34). Bottom: many paths and tracks in Slovenia are waymarked with easily-followed target marks (a red circle with a white centre).

22 Slevo *(map page 125)* ○

Car (Car tour 6) For access details, see Walk 37, page 125. 30min on foot. Follow Walk 37 to the 15min-point. Take the left-hand fork and follow this track until you reach open pasture. *On the lower slopes of Kamniški Vrh enjoy the wide, open space and views across to the church of Sv. Florjan at Zakal.*

23 Robanov Kot *(map page 128, nearby photograph page 128)*

🚗 (Car tour 6) For access details, see Walk 38, page 127. a) 17min on foot. Follow Walk 38 to the 17min-point. Picnic under the trees, or on the edge of the riverbed. *A very peaceful spot with superb views of this enchanting valley.* b) 30min on foot. Follow Walk 38 to the 30min-point and picnic on the open pasture. *A more comfortable spot, but without the views.*

24 Logarska Dolina *(map page 130, nearby photograph page 130)*

🚗 (Car tour 6) For access details, see Walk 39, page 129. 27min on foot. Follow Walk 39 to the 27min-point, where you can picnic on the edge of the field or in the trees. *Quiet, and with fine views of the mountains at the head of the Logarska Valley.*

25 Podolševa — Strevčeva *(map page 134, nearby photograph page 34, top right)* ○

🚗 (Car tour 6) For access details, see Car tour 6, page 33. Park at the church of Sv. Duh in Podolševa. 22min on foot. Three tracks lead off south from the left of the roadside parking where

Walk 41 begins. Take the centre track, which forks after 50m. Follow the left-hand fork that takes you around a mountain hut, to reach a flat area. From here climb up onto a tree-covered ridge, at the end of which you will see target marks (like the one shown above). These lead you up a short steep slope (you may need your hands in places) to the airy summit of Strevčeva. *A wonderful spot, perched high above the Logarska Dolina, with stupendous views of the Kamniško-Savinjske Alps.*

☼ Touring

The geography of Slovenia, which dictates the layout of the road system, has inevitably affected the way that we have written up our tours. Where possible, we have designed a circular drive, but in some areas this is not feasible. On each car tour we have started from one base where there is accommodation, but we have also suggested other places where you might like to stay.

In our descriptions we concentrate on the landscape and on taking you to some enchanting picnic spots and walks. For historical details and other interesting facts about the country, you need a good general guide (see page 41), although the tourist information centres which you will find in most towns provide colourful brochures about each district.

Slovenia's **roads** are of a high standard, but on some tours you will find short stretches without asphalt. These unsurfaced sections are generally well maintained but do make for slower motoring. **Road signs** are easy to follow, but do *not* rely on navigating by road numbers, as these are only shown on kilometre marker posts. **Service stations** are numerous, all sell fuel at the same price, and credit cards are widely accepted. The real bonus is that you pay far less than in Britain! We have found that Slovenians are considerate drivers but, if you are admiring the view, do pull over and allow the following vehicles to pass.

The pull-out touring maps (one covering just Car

The colourful port at Piran (Car tour 3); see also photograph pages 26-27.

14

tour 1 in the Julian Alps and the other most of the rest of the country) are **designed to be held out opposite the touring notes** and contain all the information you need when driving in the countryside. In towns, where the route is difficult to follow, our written directions are very specific. At appropriate intervals we have shown cumulative distance in kilometres and have included an overall estimated driving time. On the motorways, which have an inexpensive toll, the speed limit is 130km/h (80 miles per hour), but on all other roads do not expect to average more than 56km/h (35mph). Allow ample time for stops and extra time for any detours. **Symbols** used in the text are explained in the key on the touring maps.

We usually pack a picnic for our excursions, but you will find plenty of places, especially *gostilna* (pubs) and *gostišče* (inns with accommodation) along the way, where you can stop for a drink or a meal.

All motorists should read the Country code on page 40 and go quietly in the countryside. *Srečno!*

Car tour 1: A CIRCUIT IN THE JULIAN ALPS

Bled • Mojstrana • Kranjska Gora • Vršič • Trenta • Soča • Bovec • Kobarid • Tolmin • Most na Soči • Bača pri Modreju • Podbrdo • Bohinjska Bistrica • Ribčev Laz • Bled

219km/137mi; 5 hours' driving
On route: Picnics 1-12; Walks 1-24

This is a long drive, but it is quite possible to divide it into two days with an overnight stay in the Soča Valley. The roads range from fast motorway near Bled to the hairpin bends of Vršič and the narrow streets through villages. We have started this tour from Bled, as it is *the* tourist magnet, but it is a busy town and you may prefer quieter places like Kranjska Gora, Bovec, Kobarid or the Bohinj Valley. It is easy to find accommodation, and campsites are numerous.

Otok and Bled Castle, from the southern shore of Lake Bled (Picnic 2b, Walk 1)

Leave **Bled**★ (*i*▉✝▲▲△✖☎⊕ wc; Walks 1-6; Picnics 1 and 2) on the Jesenice/Ljubljana road, driving downhill to cross the Sava Dolinka and, ignoring signs for Radovljica, join the motorway signposted Jesenice/Kranjska Gora. Enjoy the panorama of mountain scenery as you speed along the valley past the large industrial town of Jesenice. The huge bucket wheel turbine you will see on the opposite side of the road was built in 1899 and used in the local iron foundry until 1986. Less than 2km beyond the service station, leave the motorway following the signs for Kranjska Gora. (If you keep straight on you will end up in Austria, the border being only a short distance away at the tunnel entrance.)

Soon (27km) you pass the attractive villages of **Mojstrana** (**M**) and **Dovje**, (△🕭), from where you can see Triglav, the country's highest mountain (see box on page 9). To get to Picnic 3 or Walk 7 drive through Mojstrana and up the unsurfaced but excellent road in the Vrata Valley to Aljažev Dom (map page 58), perhaps taking in Alternative walk 7 to Slap Peričnik. It is also well worth while turning right off the main road to make a short detour through Dovje, a village untouched by tourism; in the picturesque centre you will see the display of replica beehive panels shown on page 6.

Following the Sava Dolinka further up the valley you come to **Gozd Martuljek** (▲▲▲△✖). Walk 8 visits the nearby waterfalls. You pass numerous barns and hayracks set haphazardly but picturesquely amidst the meadows as you drive on to **Kranjska Gora**★ (40km *i*✝▲▲▲✖☎⊕M; Walks 8 and 9). If you are not stopping, you can bypass the town by following signs for Vršič but, if you need to buy anything, do so here — there are no other shops of

any size before Bovec, 45km away! Kranjska Gora is an important winter resort but is especially famous for its international ski jumping centre at Planica. Like many ski resorts there has been unsightly building, but the centre still retains some of its old character. At Borovška Cesta 63 is Liznjek House, with an interesting household collection and furnishings unique to this area. From the square leave Kranjska Gora along the narrow street beside the tourist information centre. Turn right at Hotel Lek beside the river, soon passing the translucent blue **Lake Jasna**★ (*i*✖🕭🅿), beside which is a statue of the mythical chamois, Zlatorog, perched on a boulder (see box on page 21).

Take a deep breath now as you begin the famous ascent to Vršič, a pass at 1611m. This route seems to have gained a fearful reputation, but if you drive with caution, the steep hairpins will present no problem. The first two bends are a foretaste of things to come as the road winds up through thick forest. It is fun to check your progress (each bend is numbered and the altitude recorded). At Bend 8 (✝) stop to see the chapel built by the Russian prisoners during World War I to commemorate their 400 comrades who died in an avalanche whilst building this amazing road. After Bend 10 the trees thin and the splendour of the route begins to reveal itself, with huge cliffs towering above. Stop between Bends 16 and 17 at an excellent viewpoint (🕭). There is a small military cemetery after Bend 21 and, soon after, you are at **Vršič**★ (52km ▲✖🕭wc; Walks 10 and 11; Picnic 4). A small parking fee is charged.

There now follows a steep descent for 10km. Look out for the signposted lay-by, **Razgledna**

Točka (📷) — a flat area on the site of an old military observation point. It has an excellent viewpoint indicator. At Bend 48 there is parking and a footpath to the **Kugy Monument★**, a statue of the pioneer climber and author, Julius Kugy (🚹📷; Walk 12; Picnic 5), and at Bend 49 you can take a short detour (4km) to **Izvir Soče** (✕; Walks 11 and 12), the source of the river Soča.

Having conquered Vršič, you now descend gradually through the valley towards Bovec, following the cascading blue, blue Soča. You can visit the **Alpinum Julijana★** (✿), a 70-year-old garden containing some 900 examples of alpine flora, not long before you come to **Trenta** (65km *i*△M; Walk 12). The village is home to the **Trenta Museum★**, dedicated to the Trenta mountain guides, which houses excellent displays and information about the Triglav National Park.

Continue on to **Soča** (74km 🚹▲△✕), a collection of houses alongside the road. Stop for a look inside the church of Sv. Jožef to view the modern frescoes, painted by Tone Kralj in 1944, which show Michael the Archangel fighting with Satan and two figures symbolising Hitler and Mussolini. Just beyond the village, turn left into the **Lepena Valley**

and park beside the river (Picnic 6; photograph page 10). Here the Soča emerges from **Velika Korita**, a narrow and dramatic ravine. It is possible to walk along the edge, but do be careful as the gorge overhangs in many places and the limestone rock can be quite slippery. The Soča, from here all the way to Tolmin, is a playground for canoeists and rafters as they pit their skills against the river's currents and rapids.

The valley widens and, after you cross the Koritnica, you come to a war cemetery with a huge cross, where you turn left to **Bovec★** (84km *i*▲▲△✕🚌⊕; Walk 13). This small town, the scene of terrible fighting during World War I, is now the most important centre for tourism in the Soča Valley. Here you may sample rafting, paragliding, flying and skiing, not to mention hiking! Beyond Bovec, you cannot miss the amazing sight of **Slap Boka★** (Walk 14). This waterfall, shown on page 75, is almost 30m wide and flows straight out of the face of the Kanin Mountains, dropping more than 100m.

Everywhere you go in Slovenia you will be amazed by the wonderful floral displays. Flowers pour out of window boxes, cover stairways and surround vegetable

Špik from the Hotel Špik (Walk 8)

Top: view to Triglav from the 37min-point in Walk 12 from Trenta; middle: hayrack near Mojstrana; bottom: suspension bridge over the river Soča, below the Kugy Monument

plots. Amidst this blaze of colour are neat log piles ready for the winter. You pass through the villages of **Žaga**, **Srpenica** and **Trnovo** before reaching **Kobarid★** (105km *i*🏛🕆🏔🏠△✕ 🅿⊕🎦M; Walks 15-17), set below the impressive peak of Krn. From Kobarid you can continue on the fast road down to Tolmin but, for a much more interesting drive, cross **Napoleon's Bridge** and turn right on a quiet road beside the river. You may see cows being led out to pasture and the countryside will be alive with people tending their fields and gardens. There are wayside churches and, in the little village of **Volarje**, old houses covered in vines.

Tolmin (121km *i*🏔🏠✕🅿⊕M; Walk 18; Picnic 7) is the administrative centre of the Soča Valley, with modern shops and offices. However, the old town nucleus remains, and traditions and festivals survive.

Beyond Tolmin the Soča widens out, becoming an aquamarine lake (🎦; Picnic 8) just before **Most na Soči** (124km ✕🅿). Here, if you would like a break from driving, you can put your car on the train (details on the touring map) and enjoy a very scenic journey as you are transported up the valley to Podbrdo and then through a tunnel to Bohinjska Bistrica, where you continue the tour.

If you are not taking the train, drive through Most na Soči, past the railway station, and turn left in **Bača pri Modreju**. Continue up the narrow valley, winding through the houses in the interesting village of **Klavže**. To reach the start of Walk 19, leave the main

Češnjica from Rudnica (Walk 23)

tour just after **Hudajužna** and turn left uphill to Stržišče. **Podbrdo** (148km ✖️🍴) is an interesting town. It is industrial as you enter, but becomes more attractive as you drive up the road beside the dammed stream. Beyond, climb a series of zigzags and then bear left in **Petrovo Brdo**. Suddenly you emerge from

the trees to an idyllic alpine scene — almost a movie set. You have arrived in **Sorica**! (156km †📷). Do make a short detour down to the church where there is a parking space just beyond the shrine, and a bench by the statue of the artist Ivan Grohar Silkar. To continue, take the left turn passed before Sorica signposted to

Zlatorog — the mythical chamois
In Slovenian folklore Zlatorog, with his golden horns, reigns supreme. The story unfolds that, in a mighty rage after being wounded by a mortal, he left his mountain home of Triglav and tore through the valley below, creating the amazing landscape of serrated cliffs, boulder fields and lakes that now form the Triglav Lakes Valley.

Today Zlatorog is better known by all the hotels that bear his name and by his portrait appearing on the best Slovenian beer! You will also see him posing majestically overlooking Bohinjsko Jezero (see left) and on a boulder by Lake Jasna, near Kranjska Gora.

Photograph: statue of Zlatorog at Lake Bohinj

Bohinjska Bistrica. Climb again to a small ski station, before a twisting descent takes you quickly down to **Bohinjska Bistrica★** (174km *i*🏨🏠🛏️✕🚉⊕), a small town with a large church, a railway station, and wonderful views. To shorten the tour, you could take the fast main road from here back to Bled. For a more interesting alternative, turn left in the centre for the attractive drive to **Ribčev Laz★** (180km *i*🏨⛪🏨🏠 ✕🚏🖼️WC; Walks 20 and 23, Picnics 9-11). This is a popular tourist destination and deservedly so. The views across Lake Bohinj are superb, and do not miss the beautiful frescoes in the church of Sv. Janez. Drive along the southern shore of **Bohinjsko Jezero★**, passing the roads to the cable car station (Walk 24; Picnic 12) and **Ukanc** (🏨🏠△✕). The road ends at the car park for **Slap Savica** (188km ✕; Walks 20, 21). Return to Ribčev Laz, and cross the bridge, to drive through the **Stara Fužina** (190km 🏠✕M; Walks 22 and 23; Picnic 10). You pass the ancient barns of **Studor**, shown on page 36 (**M**; Walk 23), before reaching the immaculate and unspoilt villages of **Srednja Vas** (Walk 23) and **Češnjica**. Turn right for Bled just before **Jereka**, to leave this lovely valley. When you meet the main road turn left to reach **Bled** (219km) in 20 minutes.

View back to Črna Prst from below the summit of Konjski (Walk 19)

21

Car tour 2: A TOUR OF TWO RIVERS

Idrija • Dolenja Trebuša • Most na Soči • Kanal • Nova Gorica •
Ajdovščina • Vipava • Col • Črni Vrh • Godovič • Idrija

144km/90mi; 2.5-3 hours' driving. Alternative route 149km/93mi

On route: Picnics 8 and 14; Walks 25 and 26. Picnic 13 and Walk 27
are on the Alternative route.

In this short tour of central Primorska you leave the
mountains of northern Slovenia to explore the countryside
around two beautiful rivers, the Soča and the Idrijca. You
drive through the wooded foothills of the Julian Alps, where
remote farms and cultivated fields can be seen on the
incredibly steep slopes, and visit the wide Vipava Valley,
internationally famous for its Merlot wines. Soak up the
Mediterranean ambience, take a siesta, and discover the
diverse history of the region and the fascinating industrial
heritage of Idrija.

Leave **Idrija★** (*i*■▲🏠✕🍴⊕M;
Walk 25) by taking the road
signposted for Tolmin; it follows
the river Idrijca. After 4km you
reach **Spodnji Idrija**, which has a
colourful and attractive centre
built on a loop in the river.
The road now goes through a
steep-sided narrow valley. Houses
and farms are perched on the
wooded slopes, which are ablaze
with colour in autumn, and
churches appear to sprout from
the hilltops. The Idrijca is very
scenic and attractive and is known
for its excellent trout fishing. The
road hugs the river and wonderful
views follow one after the other.
After 12km, a right turn offers an
interesting short detour into
Cerkno★. This town is famous
for its Shrovetide masked festival,
an event not to be missed if you
have the opportunity. Nearby, the
Franja Partisan Hospital★,
hidden in a narrow canyon, gives a
fascinating insight into the way
wounded Partisan soldiers were
cared for during World War II.
Back on the main route, continue
on towards Tolmin, coming to
Dolenja Trebuša (29km). To
reach Walk 26 to Slap Pršjak, turn
left over a bridge here, towards
Čepovan. The valley widens a

little, and at **Bača pri Modreju**
you drive under a high railway
viaduct at the confluence of the
Bača and Idrijca rivers. At **Most
na Soči** (40km ✕🍴) the Idrijca
joins the river Soča, which you
follow on the next section of the
tour. If you fancy a stroll along the
banks of the blue Soča, turn right
in the town towards Tolmin. You
will come to a place where the
river is dammed and where there
are plenty of parking spots and a
path along the river bank (Picnic 8).
Drive out of Most na Soči via a
high bridge (which the locals use
as a diving board), and leave the
river for a short while. After 3km
turn left on the 103 road,
signposted for Nova Gorica. Soon
you rejoin the Soča and come into
Kanal (55km ✕🍴). Attractive old
riverside houses give this town a
distinctive Italian air. Orange trees
indicate that the Mediterranean
climate is an influence here too.
The Soča is harnessed for power
and is dammed several times,
creating deep aquamarine pools.
Industry raises its ugly head as you
near Nova Gorica, and just before
the town there are two high
bridges spanning the river. The
city has little to offer the tourist,
so there is no need to linger. At

22

the first junction, turn right towards the road bridge, ignoring the signs for Čepovan. Just before the bridge, keep left and away from the river, following sign-posting to Nova Gorica (do *not* cross the bridge). Pass an unusual fountain, shaped like a whale's flukes, and at the first traffic lights turn left, following signposting to Ljubljana and Koper. On entering **Nova Gorica** (73km 🏔🏠⛺✕🖾⊕ **M**), turn left again, following signs for Ljubljana and Kromberk (but

Right: Idrija, where the church of the Holy Anton and Stations of the Cross can be seen on the hillside. Below: Divje Jezero, the 'Wild Lake' (Walk 25)

Slap Pršjak (Walk 26)

not the motorway signs). Soon you are out in open country. At the next junction, in **Ajševica**, turn left for Ljubljana and then follow signs for Ajdovščina. This wide valley is famous for its wines, and we can recommend them! Look out for the 'Vinska Cesta' (Wine Route) if you wish to sample some of the local vintages. Notice the picturesque little villages nestling on the lower slopes of the limestone escarpment, with their churches perched above them. It is all very Italian. Just after Cesta (97km) turn right to the walled village of **Vipavski Križ★**. There is a car park just before the arched gateway. From this hilltop village, with its narrow streets, monastery and ruined castle, there are excellent views. If you have time, explore, too, the hills to the south as far as Šmarje,

to see more Italianate villages surrounded by vineyards.

From **Cesta*** continue along the valley towards **Ajdovščina** (100km ✗🍴⊕), once the site of a Roman Fort, and turn right on the town's bypass. Follow signs for Idrija and Vipava, and then Ljubljana and Vipava. Ahead is Nanos, a high karst plateau, and at its foot is Vipava.

Pass Zemono Palace and then turn left in **Vipava** (106km ◼✗🍴📷) immediately after passing a cemetery on your right. (*Note:* this junction is *not* signposted. If you miss it, take a left turn 100m further on to rejoin the route.) Park for a while and wander through the narrow streets and up to the ruined castle that watches over the small town (Picnic 14). Take the next left, signposted for Vrhpolje. Pass through **Vrhpolje**, turning right in front of the church, and zigzag up to a main road, where you turn right to **Col** (117km).

From Col it is an easy climb up over the pass. You will see Triglav on the distant horizon as you descend to the attractive village of **Črni Vrh** (126km ✗🍴). The road continues down to **Godovič**, where you turn left. After a long winding descent, you're back in **Idrija** (144km).

---

*Alternative route from Cesta to Col

Turn left in **Cesta** and head up a narrow road through the straggling village of **Lokavec**, passing a turn for Gorenja before climbing more steeply up into the hills. The road is so dramatic at the top that, where it passes through several rock arches and crosses gullies, you will have to stop and enjoy the marvellous views back down to the valley. Soon you reach **Predmeja** (107km 🍴📷;

Walk 27). Turn right at the junction, to come to a roadside picnic area (Picnic 13). The attractive road continues through drystone-walled fields and past large houses — evidently a prosperous area! This route follows the edge of an escarpment, and you pass by scattered farms and an interesting section of limestone pavement before reaching **Col** (122km). Here you turn left, following signposting to Idrija.

Car tour 3: HORSES AND HISTORY, CAVES AND COAST

Postojna • Divača • Kozina • Koper • Piran • Koper • Kozina • Škocjan Caves • Ribnica • Pivka • Postojna

212km/132mi; 3-3.5 hours' driving

On Route: Picnics 15, 16; Walks 28, 29

Slovenia's Istria is not the most scenic part of the country, but on this drive to the southern coastal region we discover a UNESCO World Heritage Site, the world-famous Lipica Stud Farm, and an amazing fortified church decorated with 15th-century frescoes. Our tour uses local roads, but a toll motorway runs from Postojna to south of Kozina, and this could be used to access all walks, picnics and points of interest.

View over two of the collapsed caves to Škocjan (Picnic 16, Walk 29)

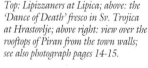

Top: Lipizzaners at Lipica; above: the 'Dance of Death' fresco in Sv. Trojica at Hrastovlje; above right: view over the rooftops of Piran from the town walls; see also photograph pages 14-15.

From **Postojna**★ (*i*🏨 🏕 △ ✕ 🚐 ⊕) follow the signs for Koper (but *not* via the motorway). You pass through **Razdrto** (13km), which sits at the base of Pleša, a promontory on a high limestone escarpment. Continue on through **Senožeče** (🎋) and then turn right at **Divača** (27km), signposted to Lipica. Three kilometres after **Lokev** (just near the border with Italy), turn right to **Lipica**★ (37km 🏨✕🎋M wc). Do not worry if you hear strange noises from your car around here — the road 'sings'! Lipica, with its lush green meadows and ancient lime trees (from which this estate gets its name), is a green oasis. Visits to the stud farm are possible throughout the year, but the beautiful white horses can be seen

grazing the surrounding fields as you drive in. There are luxury hotels here, and one of the few golf courses in Slovenia.

Return to Divača, turn right along the main road and in 2km pass the left-hand turn for the Škocjan Caves, which we visit later in the tour. Continue on through **Kozina** (56km 🏨△✕🚐) where, at the time of writing, the motorway ends. There are plans to extend it all the way to Koper. You begin the long descent to the coast from the Karst plateau at **Črni Kal** (67km 📷). There is a strong Mediterranean feel here, with vines and olives much in evidence and the houses, with their red-tiled roofs, distinctly Italian. Here the main tour turns left towards Gračišče, to visit the sleepy village of **Hrastovlje**★ (78km 👶; Picnic 15; Walk 28) with its wonderful church. The church is surrounded by fortified walls (see photographs on page 105) and looks very plain, but the

interior will amaze and enthral you. Every inch of the walls and ceiling are covered with frescoes depicting scenes from the Bible, including the celebrated 'Dance of Death', which vividly portrays that we are all one in the eyes of the Lord.

To visit the short coastline of Slovenia and the seaside resorts, the most attractive of which is Piran, return to the main road and follow the signs for **Koper**. On the outskirts of this large port, which still preserves its interesting medieval centre, take the coastal road to Portorož. Pass by Izola (there is a good viewpoint overlooking the town and the Adriatic Coast towards Trieste from the hillside service station on the bypass) and continue on past Strunjan. At the top of a hill turn right (signposted to Portorož and Piran) and then right again for **Piran★** (115km *i*🏛🏔✕🅿⊕🖼M), where you will have to pay to park. This bustling medieval fishing port is full of life and interest. The narrow streets, some supported with archways, are fascinating to explore. Do walk up the hill and along the old town walls for the bird's-eye view shown above.

Return to **Kozina** (158km) and head back towards Postojna. After 7km turn right for the **Škocjan Caves★** (174km *i*🖼✕WC; Picnic 16; Walk 29), passing some unusual walled pastures. The caves, while not as large as those at Postojna, are breathtaking in their diversity. There are amazingly-intricate stalagmite and stalactite formations and, with the river Reka roaring in the depths of the caverns, a visit to this UNESCO World Heritage Site is an unforgettable experience.

From the caves you can retrace your outward journey back to Postojna or, alternatively, turn left through Matavun and continue down the quiet and fertile valley to **Ribnica** (190km 🅿). Turn left to reach **Pivka** and then go on to **Postojna** (212km).

27

Car tour 4: THE DISAPPEARING LAKE AND OTHER WONDERS

Postojna • Rakov Škocjan • Cerknica • Bloška Polica • Lož • Snežnik Castle • Gorenje Jezero • Cerknica • Postojna

75km/46.5mi; 1.5 hours' driving

On route: Picnics 17 and 18; Walks 30 and 31

In this short tour, you take in two of the most interesting Karst phenomena in Slovenia, the disappearing lake and the Rakov Škocjan valley, before driving on to a wonderful, unspoilt castle.

Leave **Postojna★** (*i*🏨🏔🛏△✕🖭⊕) in the direction of Ljubljana. Go under the motorway and then turn right for Unec on the 914, the road running alongside the motorway. After 4km turn right along an un-surfaced road to **Rakov Škocjan★** (Picnic 17; Walk 31), a fascinating valley. Cross the Veliki Naravne Most, a rock bridge, and pass the Hotel Rakov Škocjan. Ignore a turn to the left, quickly passing the

Magnificent Predjama Castle, 10km northwest of Postojna, is built into the mouth of an enormous cave. Its setting is romantic and its history fascinating. Do venture inside and go through to the original structure, deep within the bowels of the cliff.

Snežnik Castle and (below) Cerkniško Jezero, the 'disappearing lake'

start of Walk 31, and then take the next left and then the next right, to rejoin the asphalt. At the next junction turn right along the main road to **Cerknica** (16km *i✕🏠⊕*; Walk 30), a pleasant town, famous for its Shrovetide festival. Just to the east, Walk 30 takes you up Slivnica, a hill famous for it's witches — we have yet to see any! Turn right in Cerknica to reach the famous **Cerkniško Jezero★**. This intermittent lake, on a collapsed karst cavern, all but disappears during the dry summer months, but at certain times of the year it can cover almost 40sqkm. Farmers graze cattle and make hay in the summer, fish when it is full, and skate on its surface in the winter! From Cerknica head southeast through **Martinjak**, **Grahovo**, and the pretty village of **Bločice**. Turn right at **Bloška Polica** (27km), following signs for Lož and Snežnik, to pass the sign for Križna Jama. This magnificent cave system, with 22 underground lakes, can only be explored by boat and with a guide. Next you come to the picturesque village of **Lož** (✝🛒), with its 13th-century fortified church and ruined castle. Carry on through **Stari Trg** to **Pudob** (35km), where you turn right for Snežnik. Look out for the long strips of arable cultivation and the unusual electricity poles. After **Kozarišče** you reach the entrance to **Snežnik Castle★** (37.5km ■M; Picnic 18) through a stately avenue of chestnut trees. This beautiful castle, with its moat and drawbridge entrance, has remained almost unchanged for four centuries and is surrounded by peaceful parkland. There is a dormouse museum here so, if you know nothing about this little creature, be sure to pay it a visit. From Snežnik we return to

Postojna via colourful villages with lovely orchards and painted beehives. Turn left just after Podub, following signs for Gorenje Jezero. Turn left again in **Nadlesk**; after 5.5km you reach **Gorenje Jezero**. As the village name suggests, the lake can be clearly seen from here when it is full (at other times only the reed beds mark its boundaries). Carry on along the lakeside road to reach **Grahovo**, where you turn left on the main road to **Cerknica** (59km). Continue to **Rakek** and on through an avenue of lime trees — the national tree of Slovenia — to **Unec** (66km). Turn left to return to **Postojna** (75km). While you are here, we strongly recommend that you take the short drive out to **Predjama Castle★** (■✕∩), shown opposite.

29

Car tour 5: WATER AND WINE

Rogaška Slatina • Podčetrtek • Golobinjek • Bistrica ob Sotli • Podsreda • Gorica • Šentjur • motorway • Rače • Ptuj • Majšperk • Rogatec • Rogaška Slatina

176km/110mi; 3-3.5 hours' driving

On route: Picnics 19, (20), 21; Walks 32, (33, 34, 35)

Here we explore a more rural side of Slovenia and take in some of the country's important wine-producing areas. The scenery is not dramatic, but it does offer an easy-going charm that we especially enjoy. The spas of Slovenia have long been known for their curative properties, and this tour gives ample opportunity to partake of the waters. We have used one of the spas, Rogaška Slatina, as our base: it is central, with a wide range of accommodation and amenities. Celje or Podčetrtek are good alternatives. In the main the roads are excellent, but perhaps busier than in other parts of the country. We use the motorway from near Šentjur to get to Ptuj and to Walks 34 and 35, as the drive through Slovenske Konjice and Slovenska Bistrica is slow and without scenic advantages.

Leave **Rogaška Slatina★** (*i*▲▲ ▲ ✗▦⊕M; Walk 32) on the Celje road. At **Podplat** turn left (signposted to Celje and Podčetrtek) and then left again 2km further on (signposted to Podčetrtek and Brežice). The road leads through gentle landscapes of farms along a wide valley, and passes the lovely hilltop church of Sv. Ema before reaching **Atomske Toplice** (*i*▲▲ ▲ △✗). This is a modern prosperous spa in a rural setting, with the Croatian border lying just to the east across the river. A little further on is **Podčetrtek** (17km *i*✝▮✗▦). Turn right here for a short detour (3km) to see the Minorite Monastery at **Olimje★** (✝) with its 17th-century pharmacy and wonderful murals. From Podčetrtek follow the border, river and railway south for another 4km to **Golobinjek**. (A right turn here would take you into the idyllic wine-growing Golobinjski Valley shown on pages 116 and 117, the setting for Walk 33). The tour continues to

Bistrica ob Sotli (34km ▦) with its attractive church. Just across the border in Croatia is Kumrovec, the birthplace of Tito. Turn right here for **Podsreda** (41km ▮✗), a small but lively place that holds a merry Apple Festival in October. To take another short detour, turn left through the village and then, after 2km, turn left along a narrow road to reach

Ptuj, on the river Drava (Picnic 21)

30

Grad Podsreda★ (🏛) in a further 2.5km. This impressive castle, built in 1200, has much of interest and superb views from its hilltop position. There is limited parking outside the gates, but you will come to a large lay-by and picnic area with good views of the castle 500m before you reach the entrance.

Continue north from Podsreda beside the **Bistrica River** and through **Kozje** (🍽). A series of winding bends brings you to a pass, and from here a twisting descent eventually leads to **Gorica** (72km). Take the first right as you enter the village (signposted to Sodna Vas) to see **Slivniško Jezero** (Picnic 19), the small but attractive reservoir shown overleaf. There is plenty of parking and you can stretch your legs along the banks. Return to Gorica, turn right through the village, and drive on to the outskirts of **Šentjur** (77km ✕🍽⊕). (A turn right here would take you back to Rogaška Slatina).

Turn left, signposted to Celje, and then turn right at the next junction, following the signs for the motorway. (But if you wish to visit **Celje** (*i*✝🍴🏰▲✕🍽⊕M), an industrial town but with an interesting medieval centre, carry straight on here for 11km).

We recommend using the motorway (minimal toll) for the next part of the tour, as it is scenic and has lay-bys with picnic areas and toilets. **Rogla** (Picnic 20 and Walk 34) can be accessed from the motorway by leaving at the exit signposted to Zreče and Rogla. For Walk 35, drive to the end of the motorway and continue on the dual carriageway for a short distance, before turning left for Hoče and Areh.

Leave the motorway at the signposted exit to **Rače** (113km 🍽). A quiet road leads through this village, which has a rather imposing baronial castle. Follow the signs for Ptuj (pronounced Pertooee!) across a wide plain with intensive and large-scale farming — very different from the more southern and western areas of Slovenia. Turn left after 7km to reach **Ptuj★** (134km *i*✝🍴🏰▲▲△ ✕🍽⊕M; Picnic 21). You do not need to drive into the town — turn left at the first parking sign to find a large car park. A few metres

Above: Slivniško Jezero near Gorica and Šentjur (Picnic 19); left: roadside shrine near Ptuj

(150km 🏃), stop to see the famous wood-carved misericordia in the church of the Virgin Mary, which sits atop Črna Gora. After another 2km you reach **Majšperk** (152km 🚍). (From here a detour of 14km return would take you to Štatenberg, a baroque manor house: turn right, following signposting to Poljcane. The house is 1.5km beyond Pečke.)

The main tour turns left in Majšperk, towards Rogatec. You may see storks' nests around here and wind rattles like the one shown on page 115. These ingenious devices, called *klopotci*, are used for scaring birds away from the vineyards. Scattered smallholdings that grow vines and corn have now replaced the large farms. Look out for the tiny chapel on your left in **Stoperce**. After this village you climb a small pass in the Haloze Hills, before descending towards the Croatian border once more. **Rogatec** (169km 🚍M) has a small but attractive centre. We highly recommend the open-air museum (Musej na Prostem Rogatec), open daily except Monday from March to October. From here follow the signs for 7km back to **Rogaška Slatina** (176km).

away, a footbridge crosses the wide Drava River, taking you directly into the medieval centre. The red-roofed buildings with the castle above are very picturesque. Ptuj is a joy to explore, with everything of interest within easy walking distance. Wander along the old cobbled streets, visit buildings dating from Roman times, and sample the local wines from the Haloze Hills.

Leave the car park and turn left on the main road. Almost immediately turn right and then right again, following a sign for Majšperk. In **Ptujska Gora**★

Car tour 6: VALLEYS AND MOUNTAINS

**Ljubljana • Kamnik • Stahovica • Gornji Grad • Nazarje • Ljubno ob
Savinji • Luče • Solčava • Logarska Dolina • Podolševa • Solčava •
Luče • Podvolovljek • Stahovica • Kamnik • Ljubljana**

*185km/115mi; 4h15min driving. Add another 14km/8.5mi (20min) if you
visit the head of Logarska Dolina.*

On route: Picnics 22-25; Walks 36-41

Logarska Dolina and the area surrounding this beautiful
valley should be included on any visit to Slovenia. Its
remote position at the head of the narrow Savinja Valley
dictates that this is an 'out and a back' trip rather than a circular
tour. We direct you from Ljubljana via Kamnik, near the high
summer pastures of Velika Planina, but Logarska Dolina can
easily be reached from Celje or Rogaška Slatina.

From **Ljubljana★** (*i✝✚☆✱▲▲△✕
✿⊕☺☺M*WC) follow signs for
Kamnik, turning left at **Trzin** to
drive through a wide fertile plain.
On the outskirts of Kamnik, and
just after crossing the **Kamniška
Bistrica River**, turn right if you
wish to visit **Volčji Potok★** (☸).
This 40-hectare arboretum
(entrance fee) has a wonderful
display of tulips in the spring and
is ablaze with colour in autumn.
Continue on to **Kamnik★** (23km
i✝✚☆△✕☺⊕M), enjoying the
view of the Kamniško-Savinjske
Alps along the way. This is a
delightful town full of interesting
buildings, and famous for its
decorative and intricate shop signs.
Follow directions for Velika
Planina, turning left and
recrossing the river, to come to
Stahovica (28km Picnic 22;
Walks 36 and 37). A left turn in
the village will take you to the
cable car station for Velika Planina
(Walk 36) and beyond that to the
hamlet of Kamniška Bistrica, a
jumping-off point for alpine walks
in this region.
The tour continues through
Stahovica and **Črna**, the road
soon beginning to zigzag up the
narrowing valley to reach the pass
of **Črnivec** (✕). Here you leave
the heavily-wooded slopes to enjoy
a gentle descent past immaculate

dairy farms and marvellous old
barns, to arrive at **Gornji Grad★**
(51km *✝✚✕☺M*). This small
town is dominated by a large
church and former monastery. On
the outskirts, turn right for
Nazarje along a quiet road that
follows the river through a
prosperous valley dotted with old
villages and wonderful *toplarji* (hay
barns — see box on page 36), for
which this area is famous. **Nazarje**
(65km *✝✚△☺*), with its large
timber yard, is unremarkable
except for the Franciscan
monastery that sits above the
town.
Cross the **Savinja River** as you
leave Nazarje, and turn left,
following signposting to Logarska
Dolina. Strange-looking posts and
wires appear in the flat fields —
signifying that you are in hop
country (the local beer is cheap
and tasty!). Other things to look
out for on the way are the roadside
shrines with the 'all-seeing' eye,
seldom encountered elsewhere in
Slovenia, and the many churches
in this region that are illuminated
at night. You meet the Savinja
again at **Radmirje** and, after
crossing the bridge at **Ljubno ob
Savinji** (78km ☺), you follow this
turbulent river all the way up to
Logarska Dolina. The landscape
now changes dramatically. Rich

33

farming gives way to steeply-wooded slopes which are prone to landslides, so do not be surprised if you meet road works. Suspension bridges cross the torrent, the most dramatic one using a huge rock in the river as support. A few sharp bends and a wooden bridge bring you to **Luče** (88km △✕). The valley narrows again 2km

beyond Luče, and the road squeezes between steep slopes and the river. Stop by a bar to see the **Igla★** (needle), a sharp pillar of rock that stands high above the road. Under it and around the bend is a most unusual feature, **Presihajoči Studenec**, where a small hollow fills with water and an underground siphon drains it at regular intervals. To the left is a little path that climbs to the base of the Igla, passing through a narrow fissure in the rocks before dropping back to the road oppo-

Below left: country code reminder in Robanov Kot; below right: view of Govca from Sv. Duh in Podolševa; bottom: on the Velika Planina (Walk 36)

Top: corn drying on a barn near Gornji Grad; middle: the 'all-seeing eye' on a shrine near Luče; bottom: shrine near the entrance to the Logarska Dolina Park

site the bar. The road here is particularly narrow, so take care. You soon come to **Robanov Kot**, a small village that stretches along the river. Turn left here for Picnic 23 and Walk 38. **Solčava** (98km 🚇), the next village, is your last chance to pick up provisions. The road now goes through a narrow gorge alongside the river before reaching the entrance to **Logarska Dolina★** (102km *i* 🏠 ✕wc). This lovely valley, a pro-tected park, is described as one of the 'jewels of the Alps'. During the summer months cars are charged to enter. You can park outside and continue on foot (Picnic 24; Walk 39) but, if you wish to visit **Slap Rinka★** and explore the head of the valley (Walk 40), it is worth paying the fee, which is used for the upkeep of the paths and facilities in the park.

From Logarska Dolina follow the sign for Pavličevo Sedlo (on the Austrian border), passing the entrance to the small neighbouring valley of **Matkov Kot**, which can only be explored on foot. Begin climbing the steep zigzags and, 4.3km from Logarska Dolina, on a sharp bend, turn right. After 30m the asphalt stops and you now continue on an excellent but unsurfaced road. The trees give way to alpine pastures and small farms allowing magnificent pano-ramas to the Kamniško-Savinjske Alps. It is one of our favourite drives. The church at **Podolševa** (114km) sits above the scattered community and looks up to Govca (Walk 41), the cliff-girt peak to the left. If you fancy a small adventure see Picnic 25.

Continue for 3km and, just after a

The ubiquitous hayrack
You will not travel far in Slovenia before you see *kozolci*, the wooden drying racks that dot the fields throughout the country. They are used during the summer months, making excellent hay from the soft meadow grasses, and in the autumn, when wind blowing through the poles dries the beans and maize. These hayracks are seen in other European alpine districts, but the beautiful *toplarji*, double hayracks with a storage loft and roof, are unique to Slovenia. Many were built in the 17th century from oak and beech with carefully shaped and carved beams. There are some fine examples in Studor (Walk 23; see above), still in use today and well preserved.

bridge, bear right at a junction. The road drops down past farms to **Solčava**, where you turn left to return to **Luče** (130km). Here you have two alternatives:
a) If you are quite happy driving on unsurfaced roads, turn right for **Podvolovljek**. This narrow road is asphalted for 7.8km and passes an interesting old mill, **Žagerski Mlin**, which is still intact but not working. After this there is 8.2km of unsurfaced road, mainly through trees, up to an inn at the top of the pass. Descend from here to rejoin your outward route 750m west of **Črnivec**, where you turn right to return to **Kamnik** and **Ljubljana** (185km).
b) The second alternative is to drive back down the valley to **Radmirje**, where you turn right to **Gornji Grad**, to retrace your route back to **Ljubljana** (200km).

● Walking

Slovenians love the 'great outdoors', and one of their favourite activities is hiking, whether it be along easy forest tracks through the lower hills and valleys or up into the mountains. There are over 7000km of waymarked tracks and paths in Slovenia. We hope you will enjoy these, our favourite walks, and continue exploring, devising your own routes in this remarkable and unspoilt country. There are 41 main walks (plus several completely different alternative hikes) in this guide, 30 of these in the most popular hiking regions, the Julian and Kamniško-Savinjske Alps. We have also included walks from some of the other areas of Slovenia such as the Karst and the Pohorje Massif. These do not have the drama of the high mountains, but their attraction lies in the diversity of landscape and the fascinating natural features.

Grades, waymarks, maps

We hope everyone who reads this guide will find walks to suit his/her ability. We have assigned them **grades** according to distance covered, height climbed, roughness of paths and any particular difficulties. **Easy** walks are suitable for anyone who is reasonably fit and active, while **strenuous** walks will appeal to experienced hillwalkers. Do compare your pace with ours on one or two short walks before tackling a long hike. Note that, while some of our walks require you to be surefooted and have a head for heights, none demands special climbing techniques.

All walking in Slovenia is done on paths or tracks, most of which are **waymarked** with target marks (a red circle with a white centre; see photograph page 13), red dashes and/or signposts. For safety's sake, *it is essential to stay on these routes,* which are shown on our maps by an unbroken black line.

You will notice a 'No. 1' sign on many walks. This marks the Slovenian Alpine Trail that starts in Maribor, crosses the Pohorje Massif, the Kamniško-Savinjske and Julian Alps and eventually ends at Ankaran, not far from Trieste.

You will find the **maps** in this book adequate for all of our walks, but if you wish to go further afield, you should have the relevant sheet map and a compass. Maps are readily available from shops and tourist information centres and can also be bought before you travel (see 'Useful contacts', page 41). There are two series of maps in the 1:50 000 scale published

37

by Planinska Zveza Slovenije (PZS) and Geodetski Zavod Slovenije (GZS). For selected areas, 1:25 000 and 1:30 000 maps are also available. In general, Slovenian maps are excellent (although they do tear easily), but as roads and tracks are being continually upgraded, you will come across inaccuracies, so do use them in conjunction with our notes.

The Alpine Association of Slovenia

The Alpine Association (PZS), with over 75,000 members, is a mine of information. It produces maps, is responsible for maintaining the target-marked paths and mountain huts, and can arrange guides (see 'Useful contacts', page 41).

Slovenia is criss-crossed with numerous trails and has more than 160 **mountain huts** for overnight stops. In the Triglav National Park there are around 50 refuges spaced between 3-5 hours' walking distance apart, and ranging from simple bivouacs to fully-equipped large buildings providing food and bedding. On the mountain summits you will often find a visitors' book and a specific mountain stamp, so take an inkpad if you want to 'bag' some of Slovenia's tops!

Equipment and safety

For each walk we have indicated only special **equipment** necessary, e.g. footwear, torch and, if you like to use them, walking sticks. The contents of your rucksack must reflect the weather, the time of year and the length of the walk.

- Always take plenty of food and water.
- Wear good walking boots with ankle support on all walks except where indicated otherwise.
- Take adequate clothing. Extra clothing should be included even on a warm day if tackling a mountain route.
- Take sun protection cream and sunglasses.
- Take a basic first aid kit.
- An umbrella can be very useful sun and shower protection on low-level walks.

Extra equipment for mountain walks
- Waterproof/windproof jacket
- Sunhat/warm hat and gloves
- Map, compass, whistle, mobile phone (the emergency number is 112; mobiles can be unreliable in the mountains)

Safety
- Do not overestimate your ability.
- Avoid walking alone; leave word of your intended route.
- Be prepared to turn back if the route proves too difficult.
- Turn back if the weather deteriorates; widespread thunderstorms can develop very quickly, especially in summer.
- Avoid mountain ridge walks if storms are forecast.

Weather

The temperate climatic zone in which Slovenia lies means that the winters are cold and the summers hot. In the mountains snow can fall at any time of the year, and you may find some paths still snow-covered in early June.

The warmest months are July and August, when the average temperature is around 23 degrees Celsius, but these are also the busiest times, when accommodation will be at a premium. In May and June, while some of the higher walks may have to be discounted because of snow, the fields and valleys will be a kaleidoscope of colour and activity, and the rivers and waterfalls will be at their best. September and October are also glorious months, when the mountains are usually clear of snow, the trees are ablaze with colour, and the grape and maize harvests are in full swing.

If you are planning a long walk, especially in the mountains, do get a **weather forecast** — available at hotels and tourist information centres — and be prepared for sudden thunderstorms (see 'Safety' opposite). **Water sources** in the mountains may be dry in the summer months so *always* carry an adequate supply.

Organisation of the walks

All our walks are grouped according to the car tour from which they are most easily reached. This is clearly shown on the pull-out touring maps inside the back cover of the book. Each walk starts from a parking place or from a town centre and, where indicated, they can also be reached by public transport. Most of our main and alternative walks are circular, while the short walks are often out and back.

At the beginning of each walk you will find essential information — distance and time, grade, equipment, how to get there, nearest accommodation and, if applicable, alternatives for shorter or longer walks.

Below is a key to the **symbols** on the walking maps.

▬▬▬	motorway	●▸	spring, waterfall, etc	☒	monument
▬▬▬	main road	♟♟	church.chapel	∩	cave
▬▬▬	secondary road	†	shrine or cross	⚒	quarry, mine
▬▬▬	motorable track	⊡	cemetery	⊗	mine tunnel
▬▬▬	waymarked route	⊼	picnic tables	▤	stadium
‑‑‑‑‑‑	cart track, path, trail	📷	best views	△	campsite
··········	difficult path	🚌	bus stop	P	picnic suggestion (see pages 8-13)
_2→_	main walk	🚗	car parking	📖	map continuation
_2→_	alternative walk	🚂	railway station	●—●	ski lift
▬▬▬	watercourse route	▪	castle, fort	⬩	cable car
— 400 —	height in metres	■	specified building	⛫	observation tower

Nuisances

You will find no real nuisances in Slovenia! There are **snakes** but these, being very timid, are rarely seen. However, there are **fire salamanders** that are completely harmless and numerous on woodland paths in damp weather conditions — do try not to tread on them!

Sign at the Vršič Pass, gateway to many walks in the Julian Alps

Country code for walkers

- Keep on tracks and paths.
- Heed warning signs.
- Do not pick plants or disturb birds and animals.
- Do not damage alpine huts, signs, visitors' books or altitude stamps.
- Keep dogs under control.
- Do not cause rock falls.
- Keep gates closed.
- Prevent forest fires.
- Take your litter home.
- Make no unnecessary noise.
- Greet other walkers — 'Dober dan' and a smile are sufficient!

Where to stay

Accommodation is readily available all over the country, and our walks can easily be accessed from many towns. For each walk we have indicated the closest places to stay under 'Nearest accommodation'. The Slovenian Tourist Board, both in the UK and in the country itself (see 'Useful contacts' opposite) will gladly provide you with information about hotels, B&B and self-catering establishments in all areas. Recommended camping grounds are well sited and the standard is excellent.

A note about currency

The Slovenian currency is the tolar (SIT) at present. But many establishments accept euros as payment, and it is expected that the euro will be the official currency from 2007.

Slap Kozjak (Car tour 1, Walk 16)

Recommended reading

Slovenia by Steve Fallon (Lonely Planet) is excellent. There is also a new *Rough Guide to Slovenia*.

Slovenian for Travelers by Miran Hladnik and Toussaint Hočevar. Available as a book, tape and CD-ROM, it includes conversational phrases, cultural information and travel tips. The CD-ROM has clickable words and phrases to help with pronunciation.
Web site: www.ff.uni-lj.si/sft/

Useful contacts

For maps, guides, etc

www.amazon.co.uk
for travel guides, dictionaries and language guides

Stanfords
12-14 Long Acre
Convent Garden
London WC2E 9LP
Tel: 020 7836 1321
Web: www.stanfords.co.uk
E-mail: customer.services
@stanfords.co.uk

The Map Shop
15 High Street
Upton upon Severn
Worcs WR8 0HJ
Tel: 01684 593146
Fax: 01684 594559
Web: www.themapshop.co.uk
E-mail: themapshop
@btinternet.com

Kod & Kam
Trg Francoske Revolucije 7,
Ljubljana, Slovenia

For general information and accommodation details

Slovenia Tourist Office (UK)
The Barns, Woodlands End
Mells, Frome
Somerset BA11 3QD
Tel: 01373 814233
E-mail: info@slovenian-tourism.co.uk

Slovenian Tourist Board (in Slovenia)
Web: www.slovenia-tourism.si
E-mail: info@slovenia-tourism.si

Specialist interest

Cyclists Touring Club
Cotterell House
69 Meadrow
Godalming, Surrey GU7 3HS
Tel: 0870 873 0060
Web: www.ctc.org.uk
E-mail: cycling@ctc.org.uk

The Alpine Association of Slovenia (Planinska Zveza Slovenije)
Web: www.pzs.si/

Slovenian for walkers

It is fortunate for visitors from western Europe that the Slovenians are good linguists. You will find that most young people speak some English, while the older generation will understand German. Their language bears few similarities to English, and the grammar is complex, but do try to use some words — your efforts will be much appreciated. Below we have listed basic words and phrases that should help in an emergency, and others that you will frequently come across while you are walking and touring.

We have also included a simple guide to pronunciation, taken from *Slovenian for Travelers* with kind permission from its author, Miran Hladnik (see 'Recommended reading', page 41). The Slovenian language has 25 letters. It does not have the letters w, q, x or y, but it does have three others. These are č, š and ž. The mark above the letters is called a *strešica* or 'little roof'.

A	Father or but	Š	Shock
M	Mom	G	Garage
B	To be	T	Taxi
N	Nothing	H	Spanish Juan or Scottish
C	Switzerland		loch
O	Horn or hot	U	Soon
Č	Chocolate	I	See or hit
P	Path	V	Vase
D	Day	J	Yes or hey
R	Road	Z	Zero
E	Bed, fat or the	K	Kick
S	Seven	Ž	Pleasure
F	Far	L	Left

— L and V at the end of a word or before another consonant are pronounced like the English *W*.

— D and Ž together are pronounced like the English *J*.

Slovenian has some words that have few or no vowels. They are easier to pronounce than you might think, e.g. the mountain Krn sounds like 'kern', and *vrh* (summit) sounds like 'ver'.

A few useful phrases and words

Hello, Good morning	Dober dan
Good evening	Dober večer
Goodbye	Na svidenje
Please/you're welcome/ can I help you?	Prosim
Thank you	Hvala
Yes, No	Ja, Ne
Do you speak English?	Ali govorite angleško?

Help!	Na pomoč!
I'm lost	Izgubil/Izgubila sem se (m/f)
How do I get to…?	Kako pridem do…?
Where is…?	Kje je…?
Straight ahead	Naravnost naprej
Turn left/right at the…	Zavijte na levo/desno pri…
Up, down	Zgoraj/spodaj
North, east, south, west	Sever, vzhod, jug, zahod
Entrance, exit	Vhod, izhod
Open, closed	Odprto, zaprto
Toilets — men, women	Stranišče — Moški, ženske
Inn, inn with accommodation	Gostilna, gostišče
Room	Soba

Below are some other useful words encountered on the maps and in our text.

Slovenian	English	English	Slovenian
Bivak	Bivouac/hut	Alpine pasture	Planina
Cerkev	Church	At/by/near	Pri
Cesta	Road	Bivouac/hut	Bivak
Dolina	Valley	Bridge	Most
Dom	Hostel	Castle	Grad
Gora	Mountain	Cave	Jama
Gozd	Forest	Church	Cerkev
Grad	Castle	Corner	Kot
Hrib	Hill	Forest	Gozd
Jama	Cave	Gorge	Soteska
Jezero	Lake	Great	Veliki (V.)
Koča	Hut (mountain)	Hill	Hrib
Korito	Ravine	Hostel	Dom
Kot	Corner	Hut (mountain)	Koča
M. (Mali)	Little	Lake	Jezero
Most	Bridge	Little	Mali (M.)
Naravni most	Rock bridge	Lower	Spodnji (Sp.)
Planina	Alpine pasture	Middle	Srednja (Sr.)
Po	On/upon/by	Mountain	Gora
Pod	Under/below	On/upon/by	Po
Pot	Path/trail	Pass/saddle/col	Sedlo
Potok	Stream	Path/trail	Pot
Pri	At/by/near	Ravine	Korito
Razglednik	Viewpoint	River	Reka
Reka	River	Road	Cesta
Sedlo	Pass/saddle/col	Rock bridge	Naravni most
Slap	Waterfall	Stream	Potok
Soteska	Gorge	Street	Ulica
Sp. (Spodnji)	Lower	Summit	Vrh
Sr. (Srednja)	Middle	Under/below	Pod
Ulica	Street	Upper	Zgornji (Zg.)
Vrh	Summit	Valley	Dolina
V. (Veliki)	Great	Viewpoint	Razglednik
Zg. (Zgornji)	Upper	Waterfall	Slap

1 CIRCUIT OF LAKE BLED

See also photograph page 16
Distance/time: 6.5km/4mi; 2h10min
Grade: an easy stroll except for the climb up to the viewpoint
Equipment: see page 38; walking shoes. Refreshments available at several places around Lake Bled
How to get there: 🚌 or 🚐 to Bled
Nearest accommodation: Bled

Just as every Slovenian should climb Triglav if he is a true patriot, so should every visitor take this classic walk. This is one of the most beautiful lakes in the world — a magnet for poets, artists and lovers as well as those people who live too hectic a life. Absorb the timeless beauty, the ever-changing light playing on the water, and the tranquillity of an easy, gentle stroll that relaxes the mind and soothes the soul. Tip: this walk is no secret, and on a lovely summer's day literally hundreds of people will make the circuit. So get up early, see the sunrise, and have it all to yourselves.

Start out from the SKB BANKA BUILDING in **Bled**: cross LJUBLJAN-SKA CESTA, go down the steps opposite, and turn right along SVOBODE CESTA. After a few metres you pass the TOURIST INFORMATION CENTRE and the CASINO on your left. Descend the steps to the right of the tall sign for the casino. Follow the shore path to the right

(anticlockwise) through the park, towards the steep cliffs on which Bled Castle is perched. The starting positions and lanes for the rowing competitions stretch out across **Lake Bled** from here, and it is lovely to sit and watch the rowers (Picnic 1). Soon you pass a JETTY where you could board a *pletna* (Slovenian-style gondola) to visit the island of Otok and the Church of the Assumption. On reaching a SWIMMING POOL and boat rental complex (**9min**), go up the path to the right, to an asphalt road (with restricted access for cars). Directly opposite is a signposted path to Bled Castle (**12min**). Turn left along the road, walking under chestnut trees and passing two rather grand houses. The first belongs to the Triglav National Park, the second is a private house called ZLATOROG VILLA (**18min**), with that famous chamois on the front (see box on page 21).

Lake Bled: view to the castle from the town, with a pletna *in the foreground*

The island of Otok, with the Church of the Assumption, and Bled Castle, from the Osojnica viewpoint (Picnic 2a)

In another nine minutes you cross a little bridge just before the ROWING CENTRE. The path goes in front of the buildings and by the statue of a rower. Continue through the shady trees to pass the rowers' finishing line and grandstand. You are now at the far end of the lake, where there is a grassy picnic area and opposite, a shop, bar, ice cream stall and CAMPSITE (**37min**).

Keep along the shore (perhaps stopping to hire a rowing boat), to come to a few wooden steps. This is the start of a boardwalk that offers marvellous views across to Otok and Bled. Back on the path beside the road, you reach the entrance to the PENSION BOMI (**46min**). Take the path (beside a bench) signposted 'OSOJNICA'; it climbs behind the pension and up the steep wooded hillside to two fine viewpoints overlooking Lake Bled and the surrounding mountains. It is steep, and near the top there is a flight of metal steps that climb at a dizzying angle to the first viewpoint. The second, and we think better, VIEWPOINT is only

a few minutes further up through the trees (**1h15min**; Picnic 2a). Return to the road (**1h40min**) and continue around the lake, passing our favourite lakeside viewpoint, just where the path leaves the road. A perfectly-situated 'LOVERS SEAT' looks out over the lake towards Otok and the castle (Picnic 2b).

Soon you go through a gateway in a high wall and, where the path narrows, you will encounter artists offering their work for sale (but they do not hassle you). You pass the lakeside entrance to Vila Bled and carry on through another gateway to reach the busy village of **Mlino** (**1h55min**). The many *pletnas* here make this a colourful scene.

The path now follows the road closely all the way back to Bled, passing several viewpoints. By the GRAND HOTEL TOPLICE fork left, to take the path in front of the hotel and complete your circuit of the lake. Steps either side of the CASINO will lead you back to your starting point in **Bled** (**2h10min**).

Distance/time: 13.5km/8.4mi; 3h56min
Grade: easy; on good paths, tracks and roads. One steep climb of 220m/720ft to Kupljenik.
Equipment: see page 38; walking shoes
How to get there: 🚗 or 🚌 to Bled
Nearest accommodation: Bled
Short walk: Bled — Selo — Mlino — Bled. 5.5km/3.4mi; 1h43min. Grade and equipment as above. Follow the main walk to the Y-junction before the bridge

over the Sava Bohinjka. Take the right fork and follow the track that winds through the fields where you may see the mobile beehive shown in the box on page 48. After four minutes, when you come to another Y-junction, bear right, following signs for Mlino and Obroč. Seven minutes later, at a multiple junction, bear right uphill (still signposted for Mlino and Obroč), to soon meet a track merging from the left. You have now rejoined the main walk at the 3h18min-point.

Explore all that is best in rural Slovenia. The changing colours of the seasons make this a walk for any time of year. The fresh green of the spring hay meadows gives way to the bright hues of summer harvest, but our favourite time is autumn, when the apples are picked and the countryside is bathed in a golden light.

Start the walk in **Bled** from the SKB BANKA BUILDING. Walk up the busy main road, LJUBLJANSKA CESTA, away from the lake, with the shopping centre on your right. Turn right along CANKARJEVA CESTA to pass the Kompass Hotel. Continue up the road by some fine old houses, ignoring a right turn to Straža (**12min**). Disregard the next turn to Straža as well, and after a right-hand bend, you will come to a SHRINE at a Y-junction. Take the right fork (signposted to SELO). You leave the modern houses and follow the road through fields and hayracks. To your right is the wooded hillside of Straža. Pass by a pylon and, soon after, a narrow band of trees is reached. From the bench here there is a fine view across Selo to the church at Kupljenik on the far hillside.
Descend into **Selo** (**42min**), where you turn left and immediately right at the staggered crossroad, following signposting for Kupljenik. Continue down this road, looking out for corn hanging

on the beautiful barn shown opposite. At the bottom of the hill keep right, passing the exit signs for Selo. The road now changes to a wide track. Bear left at the Y-junction ahead (*the Short walk bears right here*), to cross the bridge over the **Sava Bohinjka** (**58min**). From the benches on the far side you can enjoy this quiet stretch of river.
Turn right along the track which soon begins to climb gently through birch, sycamore and hazel trees. Keep the field on your left and ignore two tracks off to the right. Continue on to another junction and follow the 'KUPLJENIK' sign to the right. The track narrows to a stony path and then divides again by a TARGET-MARKED TREE. Take the right-hand path, climbing steeply, but stopping to admire the views across to Bled Castle. Soon the path enters a small clearing, before passing through a narrow band of trees and emerging on a grassy hillside. On your left is a MEMORIAL to a young Partisan of World War II.

46

Corn drying on an attractive barn near Selo

The path, faint at first, ascends by the trees on your left towards a small painted shrine and becomes a grassy track. Pass the SHRINE, ignoring the track which joins from the right, and reach the end of an asphalt road. Continue along this road, passing a farmhouse with barns and cherry orchards. When you come to a WATER TROUGH and TAP (**1h43min**), your climbing is all but done!

Do not turn left here, but continue along the road that now traverses above the fields, giving wonderful views across to Lake Bled and the surrounding mountains. The small hamlet of **Kupljenik** is ahead and you pass another MEMORIAL set amongst four small pine trees. The houses are decorated with flowers and surrounded by apple trees, and above them stands the little church of **Sv. Štefan** (**1h58min**). You can peep inside through a small grill .

After one last short incline, begin the descent into the valley. Keep to the left of a SHRINE and pass the Kupljenik exit signs. The road zigzags down through meadows dotted with barns. Look out for some PAINTED BEEHIVE PANELS on a small hut. In early summer you may find wild strawberries — they are tiny but very tasty! Go straight across the MAIN ROAD (**2h26min**) and follow the narrow asphalt road opposite to cross the **Sava Bohinjka** once more. This is a lovely place to stop for a break. The twisting road beyond the river takes you to **Spodnji Vas**, part of **Bohinjska Bela** (**2h40min**). At the top of the hill, in the village

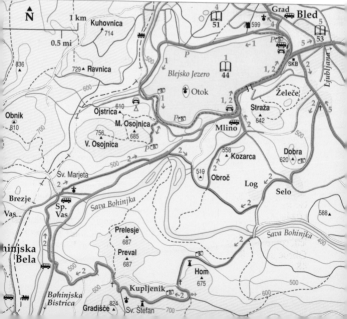

Bees like bright colours

In most countries you visit you will be able to purchase the local honey, but in few places will the bees be as visible as in Slovenia. You cannot miss the multi-coloured 'chest-of-drawers' hives — in sheds or on wheels for easy transportation. More rarely seen are the folk art motifs that used to decorate the hives. These picture-story panels are a rare sight nowadays, and you may only see them in the museums at Radov-ljica and Maribor — or the replica panels in Dovje (photograph page 6), if you follow Car tour 1. Do sample the honey — it is fragrant and delicious.

Photographs: mobile beehive on the Short walk route near Selo (left) and a close-up of the beehive panels (right)

centre, there is a shop on your left and a bar across the road. If you have time, do explore this attractive village. Turn right down the main village road and after the last house on the left (150m), turn left along a farm track signposted to MLINO. The pretty white church of **Sv. Marjeta** is on your right. Follow the track through culti-vated plots, hayracks and barns and then along the edge of the field below the wooded hillside. After the last barn the track becomes a path that runs parallel to the main road before eventually meeting it. Turn left and walk 250m along the main road, then pick up a shady track that turns off right and downhill. The track meets the Sava Bohinjka again at a bridge that leads to a military camp. Signs warn you not to cross the bridge! Keep straight on, climbing a little, to reach another track on a bend (**3h10min**). Go right here (signposted to KOZARCA), to cross a little bridge and, ignoring the track up to the left, continue on below the hill of **Obroč** until you come to a green

and white BARRIER. Turn left uphill, soon reaching another track (**3h18min**), where you turn left uphill again. *(The Short walk rejoins here.)* At the top of the hill a sign to MLINO will reassure you that you are on the right route. Emerging from the trees, you enjoy glimpses of the mountains over the woodland ahead. At a fork just before a house bear right, soon meeting an asphalt road at a group of houses (**3h32min**). The road leads round to the right, to a crossroads. Turn left down the hill into **Mlino**, passing the flower-bedecked houses along the narrow street. On your left you may notice some artwork constructed from pieces of World War I shrapnel. Soon you will reach **Lake Bled**. Turn right on the lakeside footpath, to return to **Bled** in another 13 minutes (**3h56min**).

3 POKLJUŠKA SOTESKA

Distance/time: 3km/1.9mi; 1h15min

Grade: moderate. This is a very short walk, but one which requires a head for heights and confidence on slippery ground and rough paths.

Equipment: see page 38; walking boots, walking sticks

How to get there: 🚗 From Bled, follow signs for Vintgar at first. In Spodnji Gorje keep on the main road, to come to Zgornji Gorje. Now follow signs for Krnica past a supermarket and a beautifully-painted shrine on your left. At the edge of Krnica, opposite a bus stop and turning area, turn right down a narrow road signposted for Radovna and Pokljuška Soteska. Turn left at the next junction. The asphalt ends at house No. 77, but drive for about 1km more along a track, to the gorge car park. 🚐 from Bled to Krnica. Then follow the directions below for the Alternative start.

Alternative start from Zgornji Gorje: 7km/4.4mi; 2h15min. (This is recommended for drivers who wish to avoid the narrow access track to the gorge car park, and is a delightful extension to the main walk.) Park at the super-market on the far side of Zg. Gorje and walk to the gorge car park as described in 'How to get there' above. (Please do *not* park at the bus stop in Krnica, as this is used to park buses as well as being a turning area.)

Nearest accommodation: Bled

Pokljuška Soteska is a gem of a gorge, and this short walk is full of wonderful surprises — away from the main tourist attractions, but within easy reach of Bled. It is ideal for a short morning or afternoon excursion. However, if you have a little more time, why not follow the Alternative start through the peaceful rural landscapes around Krnica.

Begin at the GORGE CAR PARK, from where a path, with clear 'P' waymarks, leads up into the woods. It follows the stream bed, which may be dry, and climbs easily up into the narrowing valley. Soon you are in **Pokljuška Soteska**. A signpost indicates a short diversion left to **Stranska Soteska** ('Side Gorge') that comes to a dead end after a few metres, with rock walls on three sides. This is the site of an occasional waterfall, but it will need to be raining for you to see it!

Continue up the main path, further into the deepening gorge, and soon you will have to strain your neck to see the sky above. At a signposted T-junction (**12min**), the names of various destinations are also painted on the cliff wall.

In Pokljuška Soteska

There is a cave up and to your right, called Pokljuška Luknja. Resist the temptation to explore this now, as you will return here later. Turn left and climb more steeply for a short distance, to arrive in a circular amphitheatre (which the locals call a 'GARDEN'). High up to your left is **Naravni Most**, a natural rock bridge. Leave this area by what *looks* like another rock bridge. In fact the sides of the gorge are so close, that it is not until you pass through them that you realise that they are separated. The next GARDEN, which has a few picnic tables, is below the 'Galerije', a wooden walkway. Climb the path up to a junction (**20min**) and turn right along a rocky shelf to reach the **Galerije**. Some may find this walkway vertiginous, but there is no diffi- culty if you use the cable handrail. The Galerije leads into a narrow gap between the cliffs. Climb some wooden steps into a dark FISSURE and, taking care not to bump your head, walk a few metres through the narrow gap out into the UPPER GARDEN.

To enter the higher valley, leave the upper garden by a short bouldery gully. The gorge is wider now. Rocks and trees are moss covered, but the path is easy to see. At first the path stays on the right or northern side of the valley but, about six minutes past the fissure, it crosses to the left. In another 60m take a path that doubles back and climbs to your left; it is marked with a 'P' sign and 'ZATRNIK' on a tree. (Be careful not to miss this junction. Another waymarked path continues through the valley.)

Climb out of the gorge on this

50

path, taking care on a short cable- protected section across some rocks, and follow the edge of the steep ground above the gorge. Continue on the narrow path which skirts the top of a slot-like gully. You then descend, quite steeply at first (no waymarks here), to reach the end of a wide path that has come down from Zatrnik (**44min**).

Turn left here, again following the 'P' waymarks, to find a path that leads to a NATURAL BRIDGE across the narrow fissure that you climbed through earlier. There is a wooden rail between you and the drop down into the gorge, but you do need to take care on the short descent and while on the bridge. Climb the path on the far side, following the 'P' waymarks to where they end (just before a fence). Follow this FENCE to the right; soon you see the waymarks again, by a squeeze stile. Follow a wide grassy path from here for 60m, then take a path off to the right (by a sign hidden in foliage and a red arrow on a rock). Follow this path (many 'P' waymarks) down to the FENCE again, which you cross by a wobbly stile. The path, rocky in places, takes you back down to the edge of the gorge.

You are now in for a surprise! The path, which can be slippery but is not exposed, zigzags steeply down and into an opening — **Pokljuška Luknja**. Inside this large cave there is a window and roof light, as well as a back door! From the cave entrance descend carefully to the main path through the gorge and turn left, back to the CAR PARK (**1h15min**).

Distance/time: 10km/6.2mi; 2h20min
Grade: an easy walk on country roads and good paths
Equipment: see page 38; walking shoes. Refreshments are available at many places on the route.
How to get there: 🚌 or 🚐 to Bled
Nearest accommodation: Bled
Short walk: Vintgar Gorge — Zasip — Vintgar Gorge. 5.5km/3.4mi; 1h30min. Grade and equipment as for main walk. Access: 🚌 or 🚐 from Bled to the Vintgar Gorge. From the gorge car park follow the main walk from the 1h32min-point to the railway. Cross the track carefully and, when you reach the road, turn left and walk to Zasip. At a junction, with the Bar pri Kureju to the right, turn left uphill to a shrine. Now follow the main walk from the 36min-point, through the Vintgar Gorge and to the car park.

A walk of contrasts. You pass through pretty villages, their gardens ablaze with colour, to reach a chapel with magnificent views of the Gorenjska plain. Then, entering the Vintgar Gorge, the power of nature is apparent. Here, over thousands of years, the Radovna River has eroded the limestone rock, carving a deep gorge. Boardwalks, clinging to the side of the cliff and above the rushing river, allow access and stunning views of this otherwise inaccessible gorge.

Start out as for Walk 1 on page 44, but after passing the CASINO, continue along SVOBODE CESTA in the general direction of the castle. After passing FESTIVALNA DVORANA BLED the road swings to the right. Continue uphill along the road, to a junction. Bear left here, passing the HOTEL JELOVICA and walk straight ahead to the GOSTILNER PRI PLANINCU (**6min**). (The bus station is just down the road to the right).
Turn left up this road, bearing right after 80m and, after a short distance, again bear right. Climb the hill, to reach a busy main road that you follow to the left. Walk carefully along this narrow thoroughfare for 120m (there is no pavement), until you reach a junction on a bend (**12min**). Turn right, ignoring the sign to Vintgar, and follow the road (PARTIZANSKA CESTA) towards Zasip.
After a few minutes go over a bridge and continue straight on through **Gmajna**, passing beautiful gardens of vegetables and flowers. As you leave the houses behind, you pass a sign denoting the entrance to Zasip, but before entering the village you walk between fields and hayracks. Ahead is the distinctive red roof of the village church and, on the hillside above, the tiny chapel of Sv. Katarina. In the centre of **Zasip** go past the BAR PRI KUREJU, to a junction (**36min**). *(The Short*

arched railway bridge. At the first wooden bridge the gorge is at its deepest and narrowest and, as you walk up the boardwalks, crossing the river two more times, you pass by a series of rapids and deep pools. Look out for trout in the aquamarine water. Little sunlight penetrates the gorge, and the noise of the rushing river reverberates from the steep cliffs. Reaching the end of the gorge you come to the upper kiosk and MAIN CAR PARK (**1h32min**).

Walk through the car park and along the road, which after crossing the river climbs a steep little hill. At the top turn left (walkers' signpost towards Bled), and after one minute turn left again. A further five minutes brings you to a T-junction next to a SHRINE. Again turn left and walk along the road into **Podhom**. Turn right in this attractive village (a left would take you past a huge water trough and the fire station). After just 60m turn left. Leave the road on a bend to the right and walk beside the PERON BAR, to carefully cross the RAILWAY. A short path on the far side leads to a road where you turn left. *(The Short walk follows this road all the way to Zasip.)*

Beyond house No. 59 in **Sebenje**, bear right (do *not* turn right down to the house) and follow the narrow asphalt road that soon becomes gravelled. The road runs below a little church and beside house No. 49, then enters open fields where it becomes a farm track. Ignore the track off to the left and, turning right, walk beside a line of trees (with a small shed to your left). Beyond a white house the asphalt begins again. At a crossroads continue straight ahead through the village of **Gmajna**, to reach the main road and your outward route (**2h02min**). Turn right and retrace your steps to **Bled** (**2h20min**).

walk joins here.) Carry straight on, bearing right and uphill past a pretty SHRINE on your right. Continue up the narrowing and twisting road through the houses, to the rough hill pasture above. The road ends at the top of the hill beside **Sv. Katarina**, with its wood-tiled steeple (**50min**). Here there is a parking area with a bar, a children's play area and also seats from where you can enjoy views back to Bled.

Go straight across from the chapel into the wood on a gravel path, signposted to Vintgar. Stay on the main path for about four minutes, following the TARGET MARKS that will lead you down to the right and into a grassy clearing. Cross this on the clear path, enter the woods again, and soon begin the descent into the **Vintgar Gorge**. The path ends at the TICKET OFFICE and café (**1h07min**). Your entrance fee will go towards the upkeep of the boardwalks and bridges in the gorge. A wooden bridge spans the river here, above a waterfall, **Slap Sum**. If you want a good view of it, go down the steps at the back of the office and cross the river on a road bridge. A path doubles back along the river bank to the base of the falls (allow an extra 10 minutes).

The first impressive sight as you start to walk up the gorge is a high WEIR, above which is a beautiful

52

Distance/time: 12km/7.5mi; 2h37min

Grade: easy, on country roads and tracks

Equipment: see page 38; walking shoes

How to get there: 🚌 or 🚐 to Bled

Nearest accommodation: Bled

Short walk: Bled — Koritno — Bodešče — Ribno — Bled. 8km/ 5mi; 1h40min. Grade, equipment and access as main walk. Follow the main walk to the 1h06min-point. Do not turn left, but carry straight on and then go right along the road to Ribno. After 18 minutes you reach a junction and the shrine shown below. Now follow the main walk from the 2h10min-point back to Bled. (Although this Short walk misses out Peči, we do recommend that you wander down the road to visit this little hamlet and its church — allow an extra 30 minutes.)

This quiet, easy ramble away from the bustle of Bled's busy town centre visits interesting and colourful villages, an old church with frescoes, and crosses the beautiful Sava Bohinjka twice. The fields are always a hive of activity and, depending on the time of year, you may see hay-making, log-cutting or perhaps, in the autumn, apple-collecting.

Start the walk in **Bled** from the SKB BANKA BUILDING. Walk up the busy main road, LJUBLJANSKA CESTA, away from the lake and with the SHOPPING CENTRE on your right. Keep on this road, passing the GOSTILNA UNION on your left and ignoring a right turn to Ribno. Instead, take the right turn signposted to BODEŠČE, opposite one petrol station and just before another (**10min**). You pass through new housing and come into fields and orchards.

In the village of **Koritno** (**25min**) keep straight on, following the road to the right. When you come to a little SHRINE on the left, turn left downhill. Then turn right by an old water pump (signposted to ŠOBEC). The asphalt ends, and a wide track takes you on across fields. After some chestnut trees and a HUT, turn left at a junction (**37min**; still signposted to ŠOBEC).

The track continues through small areas of woodland and open fields.

Shrine at the junction outside Ribno

53

Apples awaiting collection, near Peči

Keep following signs for Šobec until you come to a junction by a seat, then turn right (**49min**), now following signs for *RIBNO*. Keep on the main track; it doubles back and rises along a high tree-covered bank. At the top you emerge again in farmland and meet a road. Turn left and, in two minutes, turn left again in **Bodešče** (**1h06min**), following a sign to *PEČI*. Beyond some farm buildings and a sawmill, you come into the tiny hamlet of **Peči** (**1h18min**). **Sv. Lenart** church is decorated with ancient frescoes, most notably a large one of St. Christopher. The asphalt ends in the village, but continue down the track to a road and turn left. Soon you pass by high cliffs, a favourite haunt of climbers, and cross a bridge over the wide and smoothly-flowing

Sava Bohinjka (**1h32min**). Turn right on the far side, on a track that follows the river initially. Shortly after passing a scout hut you leave the trees; Ribno can be seen ahead. Pass a track off to the left and cross the Sava Bohinjka for the second time (**1h50min**); there is a good view back to Sv. Lenart from this bridge. Follow the asphalt road up into **Ribno**, keeping straight ahead along *SAVSKA CESTA*, between large houses. The traditional part of the village is nearer the top of the hill, where there are some attractive old houses and farm buildings. Savska Cesta leaves the village and ends at a T-junction near a bus stop. Turn left here and, at a complicated junction, pass to the right of the *SHRINE* shown on page 53 (**2h 10min**) and then take the road straight ahead (where a sign bars lorries and buses). This quiet road passes through farmland. At another junction, again with a *SHRINE*, bear right. You come into **Bled** just uphill from the shopping centre (**2h37min**).

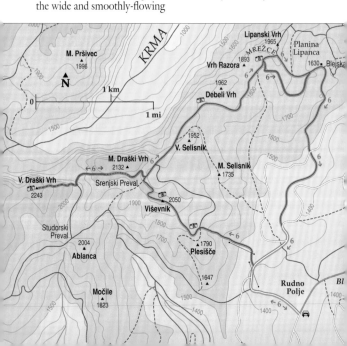

See map opposite; see also photographs page 9

Distance/time: 11.8km/7.3mi; 5h04min

Grade: strenuous, with a steep climb of 700m/2300ft. There are no real difficulties, although the initial descent from Viševnik crosses steep and stony slopes.

Equipment: see page 38; walking boots, walking sticks

How to get there: 🚌 From Bled follow signs for Pokljuka through the villages of Gorje and Krnica. The road climbs through Zatrnik and up through thick forest. Ignore all turnings off the main road; park after 11.5km/7.2mi opposite the imposing government buildings at Rudno Polje.

Nearest accommodation: Bled

Short walk: Rudno Polje — Viševnik — Rudno Polje. 5.3km/3.3mi; 3h15min. Grade, equipment and access as above. Simply retrace your steps from the summit of Viševnik.

Alternative walk: V. Draški Vrh. This out and back detour adds another 3.5km/2.2mi and a further 400m/1300ft of ascent. Allow approximately 2h extra. Grade and equipment as for the main walk, but we only recommend this route for walkers proficient with a map and compass and used to steep and exposed ground. Therefore we have not described the route in great detail. The shapely peak of V. Draški Vrh is visible from Viševnik and is a worthwhile target. From its summit Triglav appears to be very close, and the views are truly dramatic. At the 2h02min-point on the descent from Viševnik, go down a scree-filled gully on the left for a few metres. Look for a way-marked path on the right that traverses the rock face above the gully. There is a *danger of vertigo* here, but a cable is provided for support and protection. Follow this path to descend to the col before V. Draški Vrh. There are no waymarks from here to the summit, so make your own way up the rocky and steep slopes.

This walk is a good introduction to the beauty and majesty of the Julian Alps. On the edge of these mountains, Viševnik may only be a handmaiden to old 'Three Heads' Triglav, but the views from this 2050m summit are some of the best and most easily gained.

Start at **Rudno Polje** by walking up the forestry road signposted to TRIGLAV, which begins to the left of the large government buildings, between the white house and a bar. You soon reach the bottom of a ski slope. Bear right, to walk up beside and to the TOP OF THE SKI TOW (**18min**). Another tow runs at right angles from here: follow this up the now-steeper hillside. Follow the TARGET MARKS to the right across the slope and past the top of the tow and to the right of a stony gully. This path can be quite slippery after rain.

You reach a LEVEL GRASSY AREA (**48min**), sparsely covered with trees, where a sign indicates the path to Viševnik, heading left. Follow this and, at the bottom of a short steep grassy bank, ignore a waymarked path off right. At the top of the bank you are greeted with a wonderful view of Vogel and its neighbouring peaks above Bohinj. Turn right and climb again, through dwarf pine and larch, to the summit ridge. Turn left here to make the final short climb to the TOP OF **Viševnik** (**1h47min**).

View to Triglav from the Alternative walk to V. Draški Vrh

traverse through stunted trees to a small grassy COL (**2h40min**). Take a few steps to the left for a precipitous view over the Krma Valley and back to Triglav.

The path now contours around a hill, and after 25 minutes you return to just below the ridge. Very soon you come to a SIGNPOST indicating a faint path up left to Mrežce. We take this path to enjoy more views over the Krma Valley and to Triglav but, you *could* just continue around the hill until you meet the main route again at the 3h43min-point below. After seven minutes' climbing you reach the edge of the cliffs, where you turn right to another SIGNPOST. Keep left uphill; in a couple of minutes you reach the TOP OF **Mrežce** (**3h19min**), from where you can see clearly the villages of Dovje and Mojstrana to the north. Return to the signpost and then turn left for LIPANCA. Soon, bear right at a SMALL CRATER to keep following the TARGET MARKS. Ignore a path to the left after 13 minutes and continue down, with glimpses of the Blejska Koča (mountain hut) below.

Cross a GRASSY CLEARING (**3h43min**) to reach a path, then turn left and descend towards the hut. After six minutes, at a signpost, turn right for RUDNO POLJE. You descend through pine and larch, but regain some height after about 15 minutes. Eventually the path reaches a track (**4h22min**), which you cross and then descend again to another track. Here turn right to pass an excavated and FENCED AREA (**4h41min**). Keep on the main track, ignoring another track off to the right. Back at the lower ski slopes, turn left and descend to the track that takes you back to **Rudno Polje** (**5h04min**).

The view is extensive — a wonderful 360-degree panorama. Most eye catching, of course, is Triglav to the northwest, with V. Draški Vrh on the skyline to the left. To the west is the ridge extending from Črna Prst (Walk 19) to Vogel (Walk 24) and beyond. East are the Karavanke and Kamniško-Savinjske Alps.

The walk continues along the somewhat vertiginous, knobbly ridge. The path leaves the crest for a short while and then crosses it to descend a rather rocky slope, covered in loose stones. *Take care* on this most difficult part of the walk, until you reach a badly-eroded narrow COL (**2h02min**). *(From here the Alternative walk heads left to V. Draški Vrh — it is much easier than it looks!)*

Descend on the path to your right, into an area of rocky hollows and hillocks. Snow lies in this area well into June, but should pose no problems except for obscuring sections of the path. You meet a path coming in from your right after eight minutes. Keep straight on, following the TARGET MARKS, four minutes later descending a short section of scree. Do not go to the bottom of the hollow, but

56

See also photographs on pages 4-5 and 9 (bottom right)
Distance/time: 7.5km/4.7mi; 3h39min
Grade: strenuous, with a climb of 743m/2437ft. The upper part of the climb to Luknja is a steep ascent on loose scree slopes. Snow can lie here until early summer, and in these conditions we only recommend Luknja to experienced and well-equipped hill walkers used to walking on steep snow.
Equipment: see page 38; walking boots, walking sticks
How to get there: 🚌 From Mojstrana (Car tour 1), follow signs for Aljažev Dom (hostel) and Vrata, and park in the car park before the hostel — 11.5km/7.2mi from Mojstrana, of which 8km/5mi is unsurfaced.
Nearest accommodation: Bled, Kranjska Gora

Short walk: Aljažev Dom — Prag route junction — Aljažev Dom. 4km/2.5m; 1h06min. Easy. Equipment: walking shoes. Access as main walk. Follow the main walk to the 33min-point and return the same way.
Alternative walk: Slap Peričnik. 30min. Grade: easy, although parts of the path are steep and can be slippery. Equipment: walking shoes, waterproof. Access is from opposite the Koča pri Peričniku (mountain hut 4.5km/2.8mi from Mojstrana); the path is well sign-posted. These superb waterfalls are some of the best known in Slovenia and are very dramatic. There are two falls, the upper and lower, and it is possible to walk behind them both. Walk a short distance along a narrow path beyond the top falls to have a marvellous view of Vrata, Triglav, Luknja, and the lower falls.

Triglav is Slovenia's highest mountain, and you can really appreciate the scale of it on this walk. Vrata, the long valley that stretches deep into the Julian Alps from Mojstrana, ends under the towering north face of this giant, 1800m/5904ft of seemingly-impenetrable cliffs. Climb to Luknja, the high mountain pass, or just explore the valley — you will not be disappointed.

Start at the CAR PARK: walk through the barrier along the road past Slajmerjev Dom, to reach ALJAŽEV DOM (**6min**) in an open grassy area. There is a small chapel here, which was consecrated in 1928, thus fulfilling the last wish of the 'Triglav Priest', Jakob Aljaž. You will see a statue of him on the main road between Dovje and Mojstrana.
The path starts from the SIGN-BOARD beside Aljažev Dom and heads through a green barrier into the trees. Very soon you enter an open area beside the dry **Vrata** river bed and begin to appreciate the stunning mountain scenery. On a large boulder, a huge piton

and karabiner stand as a MEMORIAL to the Partisan Mountaineers. Slovenia has many memorials to fallen Partisans but this one, shown on page 9, is surely the most remarkable. In full view behind it is the huge north face of Triglav. Continue along the path, passing some open grassy areas (Picnic 3), to a SIGNPOST. A few metres to your left are some infor-mation boards (unfortunately only in Slovenian, but the diagram of climbing routes and the Prag route to Triglav, which you will pass later, is easily understood). In this area the river 'disappears' underground, only to reappear again further down the valley.

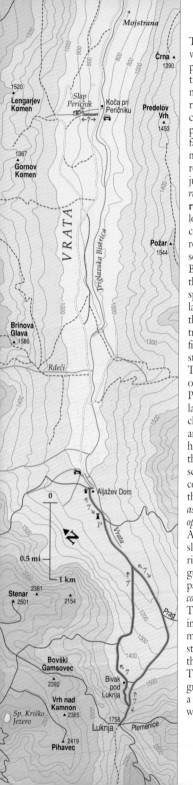

The path now enters a beech-wood, soon coming to a sign-posted junction (**20min**). Follow the sign for *LUKNJA*, in two minutes heading left, down to the river bed, before starting a gradual climb. You pass a boulder with a plaque depicting, rather grimly, a falling climber, a 'victim' of the mountain, and a symbolic severed rope. Continue to another junction (**33min**; *the Short walk returns from here*),where the **Prag route to Triglav** heads off left. It looks almost impossible, but is considered one of the easiest routes up Triglav! Ahead you can see the deep notch of Luknja. Begin to climb more steeply on the good path, over rough ground sparsely covered with stunted larches and dwarf pines. Go through a small area of shrubby trees and then enter a boulder field. The path again climbs more steeply, and you feel the weight of Triglav's north face bearing down on you.

Pass a boulder with 'LUKNJA' and a large red arrow painted on it and climb for another five minutes to another boulder (**1h29min**) that has 'VRATA' painted on it. Beyond this the route to Luknja is on loose scree slopes and you should only continue if you are confident on this terrain. *Take note of this point, as the Alternative descent described opposite starts from here.*

Ascend the steep scree-covered slopes ahead on a clear path up the right-hand side of the narrowing gully, where snow can obscure the path. *Only continue if you are confident in these conditions.*

The pass of **Luknja** (**2h**) is an important junction for many mountain routes, including the start of the Pleminice route, one of the most difficult ways to climb Triglav. On the far side the ground drops steeply to Zadnjica, a side valley of the Trenta, above which are the cliffs of Kanjavec, shown on pages 4-5. You may see Zlatorog's relatives, chamois, grazing on this lovely grassy area. To return, retrace your steps to the 'VRATA' BOULDER (**2h21min**). From here, either go back the way you came to the CAR PARK (**3h39min**), or follow the Alternative descent below.

Whichever way you choose, once back at Aljažev Dom, stop to look at the large boulder beside the chapel. If you think that the ascent of Triglav is beyond you, why not try Mala Triglav? Go behind the boulder to find out how!

Alternative descent

Take the path left from the 'VRATA' BOULDER and follow it down into the trees towards the hut clearly

seen below. In 10 minutes you reach the beautifully-kept **Bivak pod Luknja**, with piles of logs outside the door. Walk past the front of the hut to continue on an easy path. You reach another junction in 10 minutes (**2h41min**). Above you are the sheer cliffs of **Stenar**. Notice, as you descend the now-steeper path, the change in the beech trees. At first they are stunted and have no real trunk. As you go down they grow taller and, at one point, they all have a similar bend in their lower trunks. Only at the valley floor, where you rejoin the outward path, do they reach their full growth potential. Turn left to return to ALJAŽEV DOM and the CAR PARK (**3h35min**).

Slap Peričnik — the upper fall (Alternative walk)

See photograph page 18
Distance/time: 11.8km/7.3mi;
2h45min
Grade: easy, mainly on good
paths and tracks
Equipment: see page 38; walking
shoes. Refreshments are available
at Gozd Martuljek.
How to get there: 🚐 or 🚆 to
Kranjska Gora
Nearest accommodation:
Kranjska Gora
**Alternative walk: Zgornji
Martuljkov Slap.** 14.8km/9.2mi;
4h41min. strenuous; an extra
250m/820ft of ascent. Walking
boots recommended. Access as
main walk. Aficionados of waterfalls can extend the main walk by
climbing to the Zgornji Slap
(Higher Fall). Continue up the
path beside the lower falls. When
you meet a narrow track, turn left

and follow the signs to 'Slap No.
2'. Just before the river and
Brunarica pri Ingotu, where you
can sample local products, turn
right and soon cross a river bed
(usually dry). The route from here
is well waymarked. A stiff climb
up through trees is followed by a
short steep descent aided by a
cable handrail. You cross the
stream by a one-plank footbridge
and scramble up an eroded bank
to reach the base of the falls. The
water cascades over the sheer cliffs
into a small plunge pool and then
flows through smoothly-sculpted
rocks towards the valley. Those
confident in their climbing abilities
can tackle a narrow gully with the
aid of a cable to reach the base of
the main fall. Return to the lower
waterfall to continue the main
walk.

Our route takes in several of the many waymarked and numbered hikes around Kranjska Gora. A new cycle track along the old railway line provides an easy start to this walk, which is full of variety and scenic beauty. The approach to Spodnji Slap (Lower Fall) is through a narrow gorge, and the plunging cascade is hidden until you reach the viewpoint. To return you follow the Sava Dolinka through the valley.

Start out from the TOURIST
INFORMATION CENTRE in **Kranjska
Gora**: cross the road and walk
down BOROVŠKA CESTA, going
through the square in front of the
church. From the KOTNIK HOTEL
carry straight on along the same
street, passing LIZNJEK HOUSE/
MUSEUM and the GOSTILNA PRI
MARTINU. Cross over the town
bypass and follow CYCLE ROUTE
910200 along the road crossing the
river **Pišnica** (**7min**).
The road nears the main road at
one point but then veers away
from it and passes below a CEME-
TERY. Where you approach the
main road again, at a junction,
continue ahead on an ASPHALTED
CYCLE TRACK, following the line of

an old railway through fields end
enjoying good views. (Walk 9
goes through the hillside pastures
on the opposite side of this valley).
Eventually, you go under a SKI
TOW and then cross a motorable
track. In a further eight minutes
you come to a PICNIC TABLE
(**49min**). Turn right down a path
25m *before* the table, join a farm
track and follow it across the field,
to a gravel road and CHARCOAL
BURNING AREA (**54min**). Beyond
here take the left-hand track,
through pines. Soon you reach a
FOOTBRIDGE from where you can
see the gorge above two small
weirs, with the mountains
towering above. Cross the bridge,
turn right on a path beside the

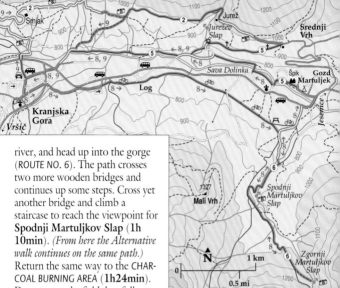

river, and head up into the gorge (*ROUTE NO. 6*). The path crosses two more wooden bridges and continues up some steps. Cross yet another bridge and climb a staircase to reach the viewpoint for **Spodnji Martuljkov Slap** (**1h 10min**). *(From here the Alternative walk continues on the same path.)* Return the same way to the CHARCOAL BURNING AREA (**1h24min**). Do *not* cross the field, but follow the gravel road to a junction. Head left and follow the cycle track to the main road at **Gozd Martuljek** (**1h31min**). Turn right along the road, over the bridge, then go left up the drive to the HOTEL ŠPIK (photograph page 18). Go by the camping site and bear left on a path past the tennis courts and hotel (now on *ROUTE NO. 5*). Join a gravel path that runs between the river and a fenced field, to cross the **Sava Dolinka** by a footbridge.

Turn right and follow a path along the river bank. With pasture and houses on your left, continue to another *FOOTBRIDGE* (**1h50min**). Cross the river again and turn left along the bank. The path soon leaves the water's edge and runs through pines to a track. Turn right, slightly uphill, to a junction, then go left (signs for *KRANJSKA GORA* here on a tree and on a large metal pipe). In five minutes you cross a stream and meet a good track (**2h02min**; the route of Walk 9), where you bear left. In two minutes do *not* cross the wide bridge over the river, but follow the narrow path signposted *KRANJSKA GORA NO. 5*. Continue straight on past a small barn, beyond which you will see a short flight of wooden steps. Go up these and, three minutes later, at a BENCH BESIDE A MULTIPLE JUNCTION, turn right uphill. Then turn left after 10m on a narrow path, to a barn. The path now follows the river bank once more. (The river bank is eroding, so take care.) You reach a small grassy area and soon after enter a field. Cross this, keeping to the left of a hayrack. Opposite some houses, look for the path as it leaves the field and continues alongside the river for a few metres, to a bridge. You join an unsurfaced road here and cross the river (**2h31min**).

Carry on by some big houses and apartment blocks, to the asphalt road. Bear right at the junction and cross the main road ahead. At the far side of the small shopping complex, take the road that leads towards the GOSTLINA FRIDA and the Internet Club. Keep on this until you see a yellow sign for 'LJUBLJANA'. Turn left here to reach the KOTNIK HOTEL and the centre of **Kranjska Gora** (**2h45min**).

See map page 61; see also photograph page 18
Distance/time: 11.3km/7mi; 3h11min
Grade: moderate, with an initial climb of 175m/570ft; mainly on good paths and tracks
Equipment: see page 38; walking boots. Refreshments are available at Kranjska Gora and Srnjak.
How to get there: 🚌 or 🚂 to Kranjska Gora
Nearest accommodation: Kranjska Gora
Short walk: Srnjak circuit. 6km/3.8mi; 1h39min. Grade, equipment and access as above. Follow the main walk past the bar at Srnjak. From the gate at the 1h05min-point, turn right downhill on a path beside the field and cross a small stream by a foot-bridge. There is an old barn on your left and ahead a hunter's lookout on a grassy bank — a superb viewpoint. The path here is faint, so head just to the right of the bank, towards a line of pines. From the pines follow a fence that leads to the left of the barn (which has 'Kranjska Gora' and an arrow on its wall). Cross another small bridge, then take a clear path with a wooden fence on the left, to pass a summer house (on your right). The path now descends through trees, dropping down a short steep bank, into a gully where you meet a wide path. Turn left down this rough route, quickly descending to an unsurfaced road which passes in front of some houses before reaching a bridge. From here follow Walk 8 from the 2h31min-point back to Kranjska Gora.

This is a peaceful walk, away from the bustle of the busy tourist town, wandering through flower-strewn alpine meadows. Superb views unfold down the valley with its patchwork of farms, across to the prominent peak of Špik and the barbed ridges around Vršič. As in Walk 8, we follow some of the local numbered routes.

This walk starts from the TOURIST INFORMATION CENTRE in **Kranjska Gora**. Cross the road and walk down BOROVŠKA CESTA, going through the square in front of the church. In front of the yellow KOTNIK HOTEL turn left down KOLODVORSKA ULICA, quickly passing a rather ugly concrete and glass building on your left. At the bottom of the street you reach a T-junction, where you turn right following the sign to LJUBLJANA. After only 50m, turn left to walk in front of the GOSTLINA FRIDA. Take the track at the left-hand side of this bar, and leave the town by going through fields, to the MAIN ROAD. Cross this and the BRIDGE just ahead (**9min**).
Turn right along the unsurfaced road and follow it round to the left, heading for the chestnut trees. Cross a smaller bridge and keep to the right of the PENSION SLOVENJIA AVTO, to begin a steady climb into the forest ahead. After a short way there is a good view back to Kranjska Gora. The road zigzags up to a BAR at **Srnjak** and in another five minutes you emerge from the forest onto open pasture (**46min**). Continue on what is now a good track that undulates gently as it traverses the hillside, passing barns and summer houses. All along this stretch there are wonderful views across to the mountains shown on page 18. In springtime and early summer the flowers are a blaze of colour and, in September, autumn crocus dot the meadows. Ignore a track that drops steeply down to the right.

The track gradually becomes rougher, reaching a bench at a perfect viewpoint, and then crosses a small stream to go through a gate. Continue on to reach another, wider GATE (**1h05min**), where the track dives into the forest. *(The Short walk turns right here.)*

Immediately after the gate turn sharply uphill along a narrow path, signposted 'SR VRH NO. 2'. The path follows the field boundary briefly, before turning sharply right into the trees. Climb steeply once more, before the path begins a gradual rising traverse. After 25 minutes the way runs along the top of a grassy clearing. Ignore the rough path merging from the right and keep ahead. The path soon forks; you can take either branch, as they merge a little further on, just before dropping to a fast-flowing stream, which you cross. After 100m, fork left ('NO. 2' SIGN) up the bank, to join a farm track. Turn right down to the farm, called JUREŽ (**1h 47min**). Take care to follow the correct route through the farm, where you may be greeted by a large but friendly dog. Go through the gate, keeping to the left of the first farm buildings, and then take a sharp right turn between the house and a barn. Turn left along the unsur-faced road ahead — from where there are spectacular views to Kranjska Gora and the surround-ing mountains. Most impressive is Špik, directly across the valley. Continue on to an unusual building (No. 5), where the road becomes asphalt and the descent to the valley begins. At the next farm (**1h59min**), on the edge of **Srednji Vrh,** double back the way you came (signposted KRANJSKA GORA NO. 5), to follow the track that starts from the right of the farmhouse. Walk up to a small painted SHRINE and take the opportunity to sit for a while on the nearby bench.

A gentle descent now follows, past apple trees and through open fields. Ignore the faint track off to the right and pass a little brown house with green shutters. Enter the forest and continue downhill. Ignore a track that doubles back to your left and go by another SHRINE in six minutes. Drop more steeply on the now-rough and narrow track, to an OLD WATER-POWERED MILL, HOUSE AND SHRINE. From here follow a wide track for 100m, to a junction. Turn right (signposted KRANJSKA GORA NO. 5) and, after 50m, by a small building, cross a little stream. Continue down the track past a wooden hunters' cabin on your right, to a track junction by a FORD (**2h28min**). Turn right here, and follow Walk 8 from the 2h02min-point back to **Kranjska Gora** (**3h11min**).

Summer house above Kranjska Gora

Distance/time: 5km/3.1mi; 2h06min

Grade: an easy mountain walk with an initial climb of 200m/ 650ft. Mainly on good paths which cross small areas of loose scree

Equipment: see page 38; walking boots, walking sticks

How to get there: 🚌 Drive to the top of the Vršič Pass from either the Trenta Valley or Kranjska Gora. There is a small fee to park on the pass summit. 🚐 There is a regular daily service over the pass during the summer months and at weekends in September.

Nearest accommodation: Bovec, Kranjska Gora

A short walk in the high mountains. In less than half an hour you have escaped from the busy Vršič Pass, with its traffic and tourists, and are surrounded by mountain grandeur. Now you can appreciate the scale and beauty of the Julian Alps, with breathtaking views all the way. Take a picnic to enjoy on the grassy slopes of Sleme, which lie just below the summit of Slemenova Špica.

The walk starts near the very highest part of the **Vršič Pass**, on the west side of the road, where you will find a PLAQUE on a large boulder indicating several destinations. Take the clear path from here towards SLEME, climbing through dwarf pine trees and crossing several scree slopes. The route is well waymarked and heads for a notch in the skyline. As you near a col, the vegetation thins and the path steepens. Once at the COL (**25min**), you are confronted by the high, bare cliffs of **Mojstrovka**, with scree slopes at their base.

Follow signposting for SLEME, heading right. The path crosses a short level section before rounding a bend to the left, from where Slemenova Špica can be clearly seen. The grassy summit, dotted with trees, contrasts with the craggy surrounding mountains. In this high area snow can linger well into early summer, sometimes obscuring the path.

You now descend to reach the headwall of the **Mala Pišnica Valley** and follow the very edge of this impressive drop. (At one point the path has slipped away, so follow the detour to clamber through some huge boulders. There is a fixed cable here to assist if necessary.)

Continue around the top of the headwall, ignoring the path that descends to your right, signposted to the Grlo Pass (**48min**). Ahead is the sheer rocky face of Slemenova Špica, but have no fear: our route will lead you up wide grassy slopes!

Look out for a path that climbs steeply up a bank on your right. (If you reach a level section and see a red sign on a tree on your left, indicating, amongst other places, Tamar-Črne, then you have gone too far. Retrace your steps for about 20m to find the correct route.) A steep climb follows, but you soon reach the beautiful grassy slopes of **Sleme** shown opposite, scattered with pine and larch trees. This is the perfect spot for a picnic, but first make the short final climb up to the summit. **Slemenova Špica** (**1h12min**) is surrounded on three sides by sheer cliffs and jagged peaks. To the north, across the valleys below, lies Austria. Do not forget to sign the book, which is in a metal box on a tree below the summit.

To return, retrace your outward route back to the **Vršič Pass** (**2h06min**).

We have omitted to mention one outstanding feature of this walk until now. On the descent from the col back to Vršič, look for **Ajdovska Deklica** — the face of a girl formed by the rocky overhangs of **Prisank**. It is a most impressive sight and a favourite haunt of rock climbers who may be seen dangling from an eyebrow. If you want a closer look, climb the little hill of **Vršič** on the other side of the road — see Picnic 4.

Opposite: the slopes of Sleme, just below Slemenova Špica

11 IZVIR SOČE • ZAPODEN • VRŠIČ • IZVIR SOČE

See also photograph page 70
Distance/time: 11km/6.9mi;
4h17min
Grade: strenuous. Mainly on
good paths and tracks, but the
climb from Zapoden is a steep and
unrelenting ascent of 500m/
1640ft. Two short sections of path
near Vršič are cable protected.
Equipment: see page 38; walking
boots, walking sticks. Refreshments are available at Vršič Pass.
How to get there: 🚗 From
Kranjska Gora cross the Vršič
Pass. At Bend 49 turn right and in
1.5km park beside the Koča pri
Izviru Soče. From Bovec/Kobarid

drive up the Soča Valley, passing
through Trenta. Turn left at Bend
49 to the Koča pri Izviru Soče.
🚌 from Kranjska Gora or Bovec;
alight at Bend 49.
Nearest accommodation:
Kranjska Gora, Bovec
Short walk: Vršič — Izvir Soče.
3.5km/2.2mi; 1h17min.
Moderate; equipment as main
walk. Access: 🚗 or 🚌 to the
Vršič Pass. Follow the main walk
from the 3h-point (or see *Note* at
the 3h-point for a longer
variation). Return by bus from
Bend 49 to Vršič or Bovec.

This is not a walk for the faint-hearted. The initial climb is
steep, but the traverse that follows — with its stunning
vistas of the mountains and down the Soča Valley — makes
all the effort worthwhile. And once you reach the Vršič Pass,
it is downhill all the way!

Start out from the CAR PARK for
Izvir Soče (the source of the river
Soča) by crossing the bridge and
heading along the gravel road
through **Zapoden**. There are great
views, but this is not the time to
linger, as there is a tough climb
ahead. After nine minutes a track
goes off left to a *pension*, but you
continue on, passing summer
houses in the pines, to reach
another CAR PARK (**20min**), where
there is a green barrier to your left.

Keep straight on, fording the
stream (usually dry in summer), to
reach a shady PICNIC AREA. Nearby
is a water trough, on which
ŠPIČKA is painted, indicating a path
leading off to the right. Follow
this as it rounds the field and rises
behind a house, before starting the
main climb of the day. It is
unrelenting, but at least you gain
height quickly on the well-marked
path. One minute after passing
through a GRASSY CLEARING, take

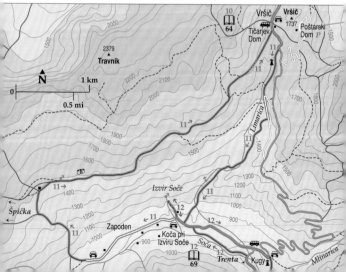

At the top of one of the cable-protected 'tricky sections' near the Vršič Pass, with Prisank in the background

the right fork at a junction (the left fork is signposted to Špička). Eight minutes later you come to another fork, where you bear right, soon reaching a hunters' CABIN (**1h26min**). Continue in front of the cabin, passing a boulder with the faint lettering 'VRŠIČ'. Two minutes later ignore another sign to Špička and, just after that, reach a TROUGH with a wooden channel for collecting water as it seeps from the rocks. The path now traverses the hillside towards the Vršič Pass, affording wonderful views across to Prisank and Razor and down to Trenta. You enter a lovely STAND OF BEECH TREES (**1h54min**), beyond which you look directly down to the day's starting point. Soon after the first sight of the pass you come to one of two short tricky descents (**2h41min**), but do not worry — a secure cable prevents any danger. The final climb is up a loose gravely path that ends by some boulders below a souvenir hut at the **Vršič Pass** (**3h**). *(Note: Should you wish to vary the Short walk and descend to Zapoden along the main walk ascent route, red marks and arrows on boulders below the concrete surrounds of the souvenir hut mark the start of the path.)*

Vršič is a popular spot, but at least *you* will not have to fight for a parking place! At Tičarjev Dom there is a large and well-furnished restaurant. (To locate **Ajdovska Deklica** — the girl's face on the cliffs of Prisank, see Picnic 4.) The return walk starts down the road to Trenta. Find a path 250m after BEND 26 that drops down a few stone steps on your right. After six minutes go straight through a small CLEARING and, following the TARGET MARKS, cross a small stream. Reaching a track, follow it downhill past a

MEMORIAL and, a few metres further on, turn left down a path. Back on the track again, there is another short cut to the right after two minutes (this one is faintly indicated and cuts out only one bend, so do not worry if you miss it). Rejoining the track, head downhill. Just after a right-hand bend with cobbles underfoot, you leave the track for the last time, following a clearly-marked red arrow to the left. The rough path descends through dense trees — very cool and shady on a hot day! You meet another track that leads downhill across a stream (avoid the rickety old footbridge). On the far side of the stream continue on a footpath which zigzags down steeply before recrossing the stream again above a mini-gorge of smooth white rocks. The zigzags continue as you become aware of steep cliffs to your left glimpsed through the thinning trees. You meet a cascading stream and walk down beside it, enjoying the views ahead to Zapoden. Cross the stream by a sound, but narrow FOOTBRIDGE and follow the path along an old drystone wall towards some houses. Beyond these dwellings, the now walled-in path returns you to the road. The CAR PARK is to the right (**4h17min**).

12 SOŠKA POT: TRENTA • IZVIR SOČE • TRENTA

See also photographs page 19
Distance/time: 11.8km/7.3mi; 4h
Grade: easy; on good paths and roads. The climb to Izvir Soče (the source of the river Soča) is tricky and only recommended for confident scramblers; it can easily be omitted.
Equipment: see page 38; walking boots. Refreshments are available at Koča pri Izviru Soče.
How to get there: 🚗 Park outside the Trenta Museum. 🚌 from Kranjska Gora, Kobarid or Bovec to Trenta
Nearest accommodation: Kranjska Gora, Bovec
Short walks. This walk can be conveniently split into two, and also accessed from the main road at several points. Grade and equipment as main walk.

1 Trenta — Pri Cerkvi — Trenta. 6.8km/4.2mi; 1h47min. Access as main walk. Follow the main walk from the Trenta Museum as far as the suspension bridge across the Soča to Pri Cerkvi at (the 1h19min-point). Cross the bridge and then turn right along the road, following the main walk again from the 3h32min-point back to Trenta.
2 Pri Cerkvi — Izvir Soče — Pri Cerkvi. 5km/3mi; 2h13min. 🚗 or 🚌 (Vršič bus) to the Alpinum Julijana or church in Pri Cerkvi. Take the suspension bridge across the Soča River opposite the church, to the information boards. Turn right here, following the main walk from the 1h19min- point back to Pri Cerkvi.

T his walk has it all! Stunning views of the mountains, swaying suspension bridges over the aquamarine Soča River, plenty of historical interest, an alpine garden, natural wonders, and shady picnic spots.

Start out from the **Trenta MUSEUM** and **TOURIST INFORMATION CENTRE**: turn left and walk along the main road down the valley towards the village of Soča. Pass the camping site, CAMP TRIGLAV, and cross the river **Soča** on the road bridge (**19min**). Here we join a trail, the **Soška Pot**. Turn right immediately after the bridge (where there is an information board in English and a map). Follow the path along the river bank. After three minutes go through a little wooden gate and in another seven minutes cross a wide dry stream bed. The path now climbs in a series of steps through mixed woodland of pine, beech and rowan. At a point opposite the Trenta Museum there is a VIEWPOINT WITH DISPLAY BOARD (**37min**) indicating the names of the mountains on the far side of the rushing river. Triglav stands

out beautifully here (photograph page 19, top). (*Note:* Slovenian maps show a marked path at this point which involves fording the river. We do not recommend it!) The Soška Pot now runs high above the river with some steep drops, but there are good handrails. Five minutes beyond the viewpoint you climb steps away from the river, through thicker pines and mossy boulders. After 15 minutes you descend to an ABANDONED FARM beside the river (**1h01min**).
Take the path that branches off to the left just *before* the farm, to climb a small bank. In another 15 minutes, after crossing a stream (most probably dry), ignore a path that turns steeply uphill and continue parallel to the river. Next you come to a GRASSY CLEARING where there are INFORMATION BOARDS about Trenta (unfortun-

ately not in English; **1h19min**). A suspension bridge crosses the river here, to Pri Cerkvi *(Short walks 1 and 2)*.

Continue to the left of the information boards and after six minutes reach a track. Keep straight ahead (signposted SOŠKA POT), to join the MAIN ROAD. Across the river from here is a telpher (cable lifting mechanism) and picnic tables. Turn left up the road, *ignoring* another Soška Pot sign on your right (we will come back this way). A large lay-by on the left has yet more information boards and some shady picnic tables. Some 180m further on the road crosses the **Soča** (**1h39min**). Turn left immediately after the bridge (there is a little wooden arrow marked 'IZVIR SOČE' on a tree) and climb the steps. When you reach the top, bear left at the junction, down towards the river. After 30m take the right fork uphill. (The left fork leads to a pleasant spot next to the river). The way is now very easy to follow through the mixed woodland, with steps in places and a bench where you can take a welcome breather. When you meet the road, turn left to come to KOČA PRI IZVIRU SOČE, a gift shop and tearoom (**2h06min**).

The continuing walk to the source of the Soča takes 20 minutes up the steep path beside the infant river that cascades down the hillside. Higher up the path becomes tricky, and you may need to use your hands in places. Access to **Izvir Soče** (**2h26min**) is difficult, and the source can only be seen if you negotiate a ledge into a narrow cleft (cable handrails). To see the Soča bubbling out of the rocks is an amazing sight and well worth the effort involved.

Return to the *koča* (**2h46min**) to continue the walk. (You might like to try a little detour along the start

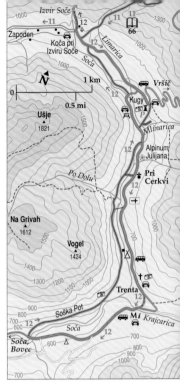

of Walk 11 by crossing the bridge at the car park and walking along the unsurfaced road for a few minutes. You will be rewarded with a wonderful view of Bavški Grintavec (2347m) which towers over the alpine fields and farms of Zapoden (photograph overleaf). From the *koča* retrace your steps along the road, passing the path that you came up on, and continue downhill to reach the Vršič/Soča road at BEND 49. Walk uphill to BEND 48 and take the signposted footpath on the right to the **Kugy Monument** (**3h11min**; Picnic 5). Julius Kugy was a famous author who loved these mountains.

The path now descends to the left of an attractive old farmhouse (please do not disturb the owners by looking too closely) and then zigzags down steps to a SUSPENSION BRIDGE over the Soča. (Here you can take another short diversion that we recommend. Do not cross the bridge, but carry on along the path to the **Korita Mlinarica**, a deep gorge. At the entrance a footbridge affords a good view of the river spouting from a fissure in the narrowing gorge. The cliffs around overhang and provide welcome shade on a hot day or shelter from inclement weather. This is a must, especially if you did not feel up to climbing to the source of the Soča. Allow 30 minutes return for this detour.) Back at the SUSPENSION BRIDGE, cross the river (photograph page 19, bottom) to reach the MAIN ROAD again. Walk downhill to another bridge over the Soča (where you met the road earlier) and continue down the road. After about 100m look out for a PLAQUE which commemorates the first of the Trenta Mountain Guides. The **Alpinum Julijana**, which has a unique collection of Slovenian alpine and karst plants, is on the left just before you come to **Pri Cerkvi** with its peaceful church and traditional buildings (**3h32min**).

Further down the road you reach a little, well-kept GRAVEYARD, beyond which lies a small World War I MILITARY CEMETERY in a stand of pine trees. You next pass a bar and a CAMPING SITE, before climbing a little. At the top of the incline, opposite a SHRINE, there is a good view down to the river. Look for a break in the road barrier 75m beyond this, where a path takes you down heathery banks between trees. At the bottom there is a house. Follow the fence on your right that leads to a stepped, tree-lined path. Descend this and then turn left on a track to rejoin the main road. Turn right, crossing the **Krajcarica River** to quickly return to the MUSEUM in **Trenta** (**4h**).

View towards Bavški Grintavec from Zapoden, near the Koča pri Izviru Soče

Distance/time: 12km/7.5mi;
2h50min
Grade: easy; on good paths and
tracks
Equipment: see page 38; walking
shoes. Refreshments are available
at Čezsoča and Kal.
How to get there: 🚌 or 🚐 to
Bovec
Nearest accommodation: Bovec
**Short walk: Bovec — Čezsoča
— Jablenca — Bovec.** 7.5km/
4.7mi; 1h38min. Grade, equip-
ment, access as above. Follow the
main walk as far as the sign for
Vodenca (just after the 1h-point).

Descend to the river Soča, cross it,
and turn left (signed to Vodenca).
Cross the Koritnica River and pass
through a camping site, to meet an
asphalt road. Follow this to the
top of the hill, then take the path
to the right (signed to Bovec),
passing through some trees. At the
far side of the wood Bovec can be
seen across the fields. Take the
track ahead until it turns right
towards some factory buildings.
At this point a small chapel
surrounded by trees is visible.
Head for this and follow the path
from the chapel back into Bovec.

Bovec is a busy sporting centre, full of athletic canoeists
and rafters in the summer and snow sports enthusiasts
during the winter months. This gentle walk takes you away
from the bustling town, down to the fast-flowing river Soča
and through countryside untouched by tourism.

Start out in **Bovec** at the TOWN
HALL and TOURIST INFORMATION
CENTRE in TRG GOLOBARSKIH ŽRTEV.
Walk down the hill, turn right
along the main road through the
town and take the first turn on
your left (signposted to the HOTEL
KANIN). You pass through an
avenue of chestnut trees on this
surprisingly-busy narrow road and
cross the town bypass, opposite a
SHRINE. Take a wide gravel track
to the left of the grass AIRFIELD,
soon passing a WEATHER STATION.
As the track bears right, keep
straight ahead on a faint path
across a field. Passing to the left of
some bushy trees, the path
becomes well defined, plunging
down into a tunnel of trees to
continue on through the wood
and to a road. Turn right, to cross
a modern bridge over the river
Soča (**24min**).
The village of **Čezsoča** is only a
few minutes further on and is well
worth exploring. The gardens are
a mass of flowers — and look out
for the little model house.
(If you do not visit the village,

turn left down some wooden steps
immediately after the bridge, to
follow a grassy path through wild
flowers on the banks of the Soča.
In less than two minutes this path
reaches a wide gravel track, where
you turn left.)
Coming from Čezsoča, turn right
on a track just past the bar,
opposite the FOOTBALL PITCH. The
track runs through trees beside the
Soča and passes a renovated
WATERMILL. At a large, wide bend
in the river you meet a road where
there are plenty of picnic tables
(**40min**).
Turn left along the road, crossing
a bridge. Ahead in the distance is
shapely Svinjak, and to the left is
Mount Rombon. Continue along
the narrow asphalt road to the
hamlet of **Uštinc** (pronounced
ushtince), where the road becomes
a gravel track lined with trees. This
is a shady stretch, but there are
always good views of the
surrounding mountains. At the
next hamlet, **Jablenca** (**1h**), bear
right, slightly uphill, through the
houses. As you continue along the

71

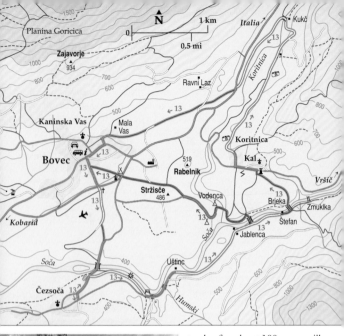

track, after about 100m you will pass a path down left signposted to VODENCA (opposite a wood-shed). *(The Short walk takes this path.)*

Keep along the gravel track past fields and orchards to reach **Štefan**. Immediately *before* the first house on the left, take a path off to the right, to cross a small stream on a footbridge. Now follow the path beside a wall. The path leaves the wall at a GATE and, after fording a small stream, enters woodland. Soon the path forks left downhill and continues above the Soča. Ignore a path that comes down from the right and descend a rocky bank down to a wooden SUSPENSION BRIDGE. Cross the river (be careful, as the bridge is slippery if wet) to the rocky promontory that juts out into the water. Here the fast-flowing Soča is popular with rafters and canoeists and, down by the water's edge, there is a sandy beach where you can paddle, cool your feet and

Suspension bridge over the Soča near Jablenca (Short walk)

Canoeists on the fast-flowing Soča River

enjoy a picnic (**1h19min**).
Then take the left fork in the path;
it starts by following the river
downstream. You soon come to a
field where the path forks. Take
the right-hand branch (unsigned),
to head up a gravel path through
some trees. At the edge of the next
clearing take a path on your left
which ascends through a few more
trees before climbing a grassy
bank. At the top there is a steel
cable, from where you can see Kal
across the fields. If you head just
to the right of the hamlet you will
find a track that leads to the main
road at **Kal** by a small WAR
MEMORIAL (**1h32min**).
Cross the main road and walk up
to the houses in Kal, then turn left
at the junction. Walk behind a bar
and parallel to the main road, to
reach **Koritnica**. Turn right at the
BUS STOP. Keep to the right of a
WATER TROUGH and then bear left
at a second trough, up a concrete
road. This road soon becomes a
gravel track and, after rounding a
right-hand bend, gives superb
mountain views of Rombon to the
left and Krnice ahead. Go through
woods, ignoring a track off to the
right. Further on, descend into a
large hay field, at the far end of
which there is a small farm with
some PAINTED BEEHIVE PANELS.
The track now continues through
trees. At a fork, keep left and then
go left again, passing a track which
heads up to a house. You drop
more steeply now and, above fields
and a farm, you come to a METAL
GATE. Continue along the track to
the farm, called KUKC. To the left
of the house is a shed, and you will
see the way from here to the wide
suspension bridge over the
Koritnica River (**2h17min**).
On the far side follow the gravel
road, ignoring a path doubling
back to the right. In 15 minutes
you reach a MAIN ROAD. Walk

50m to the left and cross over, to
take a path signed to BOVEC. After
eight minutes cross a gravel track
and continue on a wider path
(signed to MALA VAS), soon
entering open pasture. Shortly
after a curious archway of low
trees the path crosses a gravel track
(not marked on any map). At the
end of the first field the way, now
a track, runs beside a fenced
orchard. Where the track turns left
towards the main road, leave it
and follow a path into the trees.
Ford a shallow stream and keep
straight on; soon you will see
Bovec. The path runs beside a wire
fence and then a hedge, to meet an
asphalt road at the first houses.
Follow this road which has a
walled-in stream running on its
left. Turn left on the first road that
crosses this stream (by house No.
22), quickly meeting the main
road by a bar. Turn right to return
to the centre of **Bovec** (**2h50min**).

14 SLAP BOKA

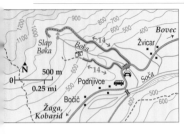

Distance/time: 1.5km/1mi; 1h20min.

Grade: easy-moderate; a short but steep climb and descent of approximately 250m/820ft on a rough path

Equipment: see page 38; walking boots, walking sticks

How to get there: 🚌 Slap Boka is 16km/10mi north of Kobarid and 5.5km/3.4mi southwest of Bovec, near Žaga. Park either side of the bridge over the Boka River. 🚌 There is a bus stop a few hundred

Below: the source of Slap Boka (Alternative walk). The views to the main fall on this route are limited, but the source itself is worth the climb.

Slap Boka — a magnificent 100m-high cascade

metres south of the start of the walk.

Nearest accommodation: Bovec

Alternative walk: Source of Slap Boka. 3.25km/2mi; 3.5-4h. Strenuous, with an ascent of approximately 500m/1600ft. Only recommended for fit walkers confident on loose, exposed slopes. *Note:* There is only a limited view of the waterfall itself on this route, but the source is a magical, awe-inspiring sight. Equipment and access as main walk. From the car park at the east side of the bridge over the Boka, cross the road and follow the clearly-marked path which goes up the right-hand side of the river. This route becomes steep and rocky in places but is easy to follow. The path veers away from the edge of the cliff, eventually descending precipitously beside a steep and exposed slope (there is a secure cable for safety), to where the river springs from the mountainside. It is an amazing sight. Within a short distance the volume of water is huge as it rushes to plunge over the precipice. *Warning* — do not venture beyond the source. There is a path, but it peters out on very steep and exposed ground. Return by the same route.

Our shortest walk, but a good pipe opener! Slap Boka is one of Slovenia's most amazing sights — a huge, improbable waterfall that cascades from the rock face. We take you to the nearest viewpoint.

Begin from the CAR PARK on the west side of the bridge over the **Boka River**. Cross the road to join a gravel track and immediately bear left on a wide path. Look out for a SIGNPOST marking the start of a footpath climbing steeply to your left. From here orange waymarks will guide you the whole way.

The attractive path runs through woods of birch, hazel and ash and between silver-grey boulders. In about 10 minutes you will get your first good views of **Slap Boka** and just after this, there are lovely views back along the Soča Valley and to Bovec.

Continue to climb and you will come to what we consider to be the best clear VIEWPOINT of this magnificent waterfall (**45min**). The river, which seems to appear from nowhere, drops in a 100m-high fall and then cascades down the rocks into the chasm below. In the morning, when the shadows move off the falls, the sunlight produces different colour effects and shades on the water — it is a wonderful sight.

Return by the same route to the CAR PARK (**1h20min**).

See also photograph page 82
Distance/time: 11.8km/7.3mi; 7h29min
Grade: very strenuous, with a total ascent of 1360m/4460ft. The whole walk is waymarked, but *we only recommend it for walkers who have map reading and compass skills.* At the summit, if weather conditions have deteriorated or you find that the ascent has taken longer than expected, we recommend that you retrace your steps. The continuation of the walk is committing; *there are no short cuts.*
Equipment: see page 38; walking boots, walking sticks
How to get there: 🚌 From Kobarid, cross the Soča on

Napoleon's Bridge and then head downstream to Ladra. Here turn left and drive through Smast, Libušnje and Vrsno to reach Krn. Turn left in this tiny hamlet and drive to the end of the road, where there is parking space on the Planina Kuhinja. The road above Vrsno is particularly narrow, so drive carefully.
Nearest accommodation: Kobarid
Short walk: Viewpoint above Planina Zaslap. 5.3km/3.3mi; 2h55min. Moderate, with 600m/ 2000ft of ascent. Equipment and access as main walk. Follow the main walk to the 1h37min-point and return the same way.

This is one of our favourite days out. The slopes of Krn — one huge alpine pasture, almost devoid of trees and with sweeping vistas — are a place of timeless tranquillity. Here the only sounds you will hear are cowbells, birdsong and the tumbling of water, and occasionally the chiming of a distant church bell. This is a long walk, but if you are in need of spiritual renewal do not miss it.

Start out from the CAR PARK on the **Planina Kuhinja** by taking the left-hand track down through a GATE and over a BRIDGE. About one minute later, bear right and head along a grassy track that leads to another GATE. Below and to your left is a *koča*. These lower slopes of Krn are excellent pasture and have been fenced to form large paddocks. Please shut all the gates behind you. The doe-eyed cows are amazingly friendly and the chime of their cowbells will accompany you as you progress. Look out for the TARGET MARKS that will guide you for the whole day. The path now heads up towards the trees and through a GATE. Beyond the gate, make sure that you take the right-hand fork. You soon cross a gravel track and enter another paddock. The clear

and well-worn path climbs steadily above a stream on the right and gives little respite until you reach the dairy sheds and the herdsman's house at **Planina Slapnik**. Go through another gate, to a large WATER TROUGH in front of the buildings (**35min**), where you may meet the friendly herdsman watching his cows and your progress!
To the right of the house is a gate. Go through this and climb steeply uphill on the path to your left. You will cross the track three more times; at the third crossing (**53min**) the buildings of **Planina Zaslap** can be seen on the left. Continue up just as steeply for a short while, before meeting a faint path on the left. Turn *right* here and enjoy the easier gradient. The path completes a long rising

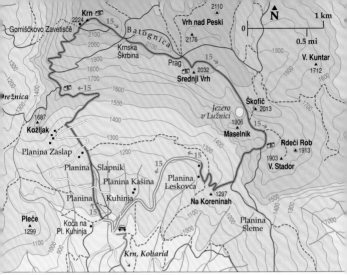

traverse, before bending sharply to the left and returning across the hillside to a *GRASSY SHOULDER* (**1h37min**). There is a wonderful view here to the Soča Valley, with its backdrop of countless hills stretching into Italy. Directly below is Drežnica, a little alpine village with a pretty white church. *(The Short walk turns back here.)*
Krn is a very deceptive mountain and you may think that you are nearly there — after all, you can see the hut just below the top. Do not be fooled; you still have 600m to climb to the summit and approximately 2h more to go! But the way from here is clear and easily followed as it gradually zigzags its way to the summit on an old wartime path. Not far past the shoulder, ignore a path that heads off right across the broad slopes and climbs to the Krnska Škrbina col. Higher up, again ignore a fainter path that heads left, across the difficult western side of Krn. Eventually, and after much effort, you reach the mountain hut of **Gomiščkovo Zavetišče** (**3h37min**). It is only manned at weekends and holidays, but the outer door is open and the shelter may be welcome.
Continue on to the top — there are still 62m to go! A multitude of paths lead up to the summit over steep slopes of scree and rocks. The panorama from the *SUMMIT OF* **Krn** (**3h52min**) is simply stunning. The main massif of the Julian Alps dominates to the north, while to the south the landscapes are the undulating and wooded hills of the Karst. The excellent viewpoint indicator will help you get your bearings. Descend southeast from the summit towards a little col, passing through a mass of barbed wire, remaining evidence of the fierce fighting that took place during Word War I on the Izonzo Front. (From just above the col a path heads right, crossing the slopes to rejoin your ascent route just above the grassy shoulder.) From the far side of the col (**Krnska Škrbina; 4h07min**) a flight of steps takes you up through World War I army defences and shelters. Some are tunnelled right through the mountain and look out to the other side of the ridge. Can you imagine the hardships the soldiers endured through the long winters? The path finally climbs on to the ridge of **Batognica** and then circles above steep escarpments,

Left: a barbed-wire cross on the climb to the Batognica ridge; below left: cows on the lower slopes of Krn; bottom: view northeast from Krn summit, down to Krnsko Jezero

hole. But continue along the valley floor to eventually reach a small circular pool, **Jezero v Lužnici** (**5h22min**).

Take the path from the far side of the pool. It climbs the grassy hillside to a low col, then descends again. While threading your route around the huge boulders, consider where they came from and look up to see areas of clean rock on the cliffs above — evidence of recent rock falls. The path continues around to the right and brings you to the top of a steep slope and a wonderful VIEWPOINT. From here it zigzags down, before heading left onto a sloping ridge and descending again to **Planina Leskovca** (**7h02min**), a collection of old huts and two modern farm buildings.

Take the track from here, passing through a gate after five minutes. Continue along a grassy ridge and through another gate before swinging to the right and descending again. Opposite a house surrounded by trees you may encounter groups of friendly ponies and more cows. Soon you cross a cattle grid to go through another gate, and in two minutes you are back at the CAR PARK at **Planina Kuhinja** (**7h29min**).

passing many more shelters. You then descend via a trench hewn from the rocks to the exposed and barren col of **Prag** (**4h37min**). Take your last look north at the Julian Alps, before you drop into the high stony valley to your right. The path now follows a ridge for a short way before zigzagging down the steep slopes to the valley floor. You may feel completely hemmed in, with no way out of this rocky

See also photos on pages 41, 82
Distance/time: 6km/3.8mi;
1h53min
Grade: easy; on good but
occasionally steep paths and tracks
Equipment: see page 38; walking
boots. Refreshments are available
at Kamp Lazar.
How to get there: 🚗 or 🚌 to
Kobarid
Nearest accommodation: Kobarid
Short walk: Slap Kozjak. 5km/

3.1mi; 1h20min. Grade, equip-
ment and access as main walk.
Walk via Napoleon's Bridge to
Slap Kozjak (the main walk in
reverse). To return, either retrace
your steps or cross the Soča on the
suspension bridge and turn left on
Napoleon's Road, to walk past
Kamp Lazar. The road then runs
high above the river to Napoleon's
Bridge and the road back to
Kobarid.

The futility of trench warfare and the hardships that the
ordinary soldier endured become all too apparent on this
walk around Kobarid. The town is home to a famous
museum, where the horrors of World War I in this area are
well documented. Above the town stands a charnel house, the
final resting place of 7014 Italian soldiers. But, away from
memories of the past, this is a pleasant woodland walk that
crosses the Soča and explores a hidden waterfall, Slap Kozjak.

Start out in Kobarid: with your
back to the MUSEUM, turn left
along the main street, passing a
sports shop, towards the town
centre. As you reach the SQUARE,
turn right uphill between two
large STONE PILLARS. The hedge-
lined asphalt road climbs steadily
up past the Stations of the Cross
to the church of Sv. Anton and
CHARNEL HOUSE shown on page
82 (13min). Take the good track
leading up to the left of, and
beside, the first storey of the
charnel house; it levels off and
heads into the trees. A short way
into the wood, branch left on the
clearly-signed path that climbs a
little bank. RED ARROWS guide you
on this walk. The path meanders
through the open wood, and
carpeting the floor in places are
patches of tiny pink cyclamen.
When you pass a walled enclosure
you meet another path merging
from the left. Turn right here on
an old cobbled trail alongside a
wall, and ignore any paths off to
the left or right. At one point there
is a lovely view of the hamlets of
Magozd and Jezerca across the

valley, below the steep slopes of
Krn. One minute after passing an
old tin-roofed HUT in a grassy
clearing, there is a picnic table set
in a stand of fine beech trees. Soon
you will see your next objective,
Tonocov Grad, but unfortunately
you have to drop all the way down
to cross the stream before
climbing the hill.
One minute from the stream keep
right at a junction, and then, two
minutes later, fork right to reach
the SUMMIT OF Tonocov Grad
(40min). At the top of the
wooden steps there is a large
multi-lingual information board
detailing the historical importance
of the site; archaeological work is
still being carried out here. The
view from the top looks south
over the Soča Valley and back to
the charnel house and Sv. Anton.
Retrace your steps to the junction
at the bottom of the wooden steps
and turn right. The path contours
the hill before descending more
steeply. You will come to a large
World War I CONCRETE TRENCH
(part of the Italian 3rd Defence

Line) on the right. Enter this to descend to the road by steep steps, using the cable handrail if necessary. (We think this is safer than the route that bypasses the trench, as the steps have crumbled in places). Cross the road, turn left and drop again on a stepped path. At one point you walk through another WARTIME TRENCH, before reaching a track called **Napoleon's Road** (58min). Turn right here, and after about 100m turn left beside an INFORMATION BOARD and large dug-out, to make the final short descent to the **Soča**. On the far side of the SUSPENSION BRIDGE, turn left up a stony track.

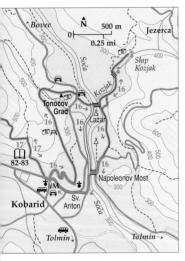

After seven minutes you cross a STONE BRIDGE that spans a deep gorge and a waterfall. Bear right just after this (clearly signposted) to follow the bank upstream. The path ends at the water's edge, where you cross a wooden bridge that leads to a paved path up the stream bed. To reach the waterfall viewing platform you must first edge along a path (with a secure cable) hewn into the rock face. Some walkers may find this difficult, but **Slap Kozjak** (1h13min; photograph page 41) is well worth the effort. (If the water is shallow enough, you *may* be able to see the falls by paddling up the stream, thereby avoiding the rock shelf.) The water gushes from a spout and falls into a deep, beautifully coloured pool in a rocky cavern. Return the same way. Two minutes past the STONE BRIDGE, on a sharp bend to the left, take a path which heads uphill to the left, past TRENCHES even more extensive than those seen before. A myriad of paths lets you explore gun emplacements, observation points and shelters tunnelled into the rocks. Follow the path through the centre of this area to return to the track. Turn left and follow the Soča downstream.

The track climbs away from the river, passes through some fields and joins an asphalt road. Turn right here, past the entrance to KAMP KOREN, and walk down to **Napoleon's Bridge** (1h44min), spanning the Soča above a beautiful narrow gorge. Cross over and turn left uphill on the road. Ignoring a road to the left, you come to a junction. The main road through the Soča Valley merges here, so take care as you return down the narrow street past flower-decorated houses, to the MUSEUM in **Kobarid** (1h53min).

Napoleon's Bridge over the river Soča

Distance/time: 24km/15mi; 7h20min
Grade: very strenuous. A long walk, with a total ascent and descent of 1460m/4790ft.
Equipment: see page 38; walking boots, walking sticks
How to get there: 🚗 or 🚐 to Kobarid

Nearest accommodation: Kobarid
Short walk: Starijski Vrh. 7km/4.3mi; 3h30min. Strenuous (ascent/descent of 950m/3120ft); equipment and access as main walk. Follow the main walk to the 1h58min-point; return the same way.

An unrelenting, steep climb — for the very fit — is rewarded with stunning views along and across the Soča Valley to the peaks of the Julian Alps. The long easy ridge of Stol stretches out ahead, with the summit and more wonderful panoramas beckoning you on.

Start the walk from the main square in **Kobarid** by the RESTAURANT KATLAR. Opposite there is a sign, 'STOL 4 URA' (Stol 4h), pointing towards a narrow cobbled lane through some pretty flower-decorated houses. Start the ascent here, and soon you are walking on an old cobbled trail. The whole route is well waymarked with TARGET MARKS and red flashes. The climb is steep and relentless, through a green and grey world of trees and limestone boulders, with shafts of sunshine piercing the canopy above. Kobarid, and the noise of town life are very quickly left behind, and all you can hear are woodland sounds … and your own heavy breathing!

Eventually you rise to an old tin-roofed HUT (**54min**) and, six minutes later, you reach a small GRASSY CLEARING with the first views down to the valley below. On entering the woodland again another sign, 'STOL 3 URA', tells you that your goal is now only three hours away. Continue on a narrow path past a white building, soon joining the cobbled trail once more. It turns left, passing another old HUT (**1h20min**). Just after this hut, turn left and climb even more steeply up a dirt path over tree roots. On this slope watch for the DIAGONAL STRIPE ON A BOULDER, indicating a right turn. Soon, another little CLEARING is reached. Stop here to look back to the jagged northwest ridge and

View along Stol's lengthy ridge from near the summit

pointed peak of Krn. From the clearing the path bears right into the trees again, and your next clear landmark is a *ROCKY RIDGE* which you follow, sometimes along the crest, to the grassy top of **Starijski Vrh** (**1h58min**). You have worked hard for a well-earned rest and this is a wonderful spot to relax for a while and take in the views all around. *(The Short walk returns from here.)*

However, the distant peak of Stol still beckons. Follow the path through the rough grazing along the broad ridge, to a track where a sign on a tree tells you that Stol is two hours away ('STOL 2 URA'; (**2h10min**).

Continue along this track that hugs the southern side of the ridge above very steep slopes. After four minutes the track bends sharply to the right, but you should continue straight on up the bank (a clearly-waymarked short cut). A second short cut misses out another bend and, after 100m, you come to the FIRST METAL GATE. Please make sure you fasten all the gates. The route along the ridge is easy with only a gradual ascent — in fact, for part of the way you may feel that you are walking along a leafy country lane. From the second gate you will see a bench on the distant skyline. The track runs just below this and round the corner is the **Lovska Koča** mountain hut (**2h28min**).

After the third gate you leave the trees and begin a stretch on open hillside, soon passing a little cabin called **Bivak Hlek** where there is a trough and a tap. (Slovenian maps show a waymarked path descending from here to the valley. We have searched for this but could find no trace, so please do not rely on it as a way back to Kobarid.) After 25 minutes you come to yet another gate and, two gates later, you reach a welcome picnic table

and a clearly SIGNPOSTED JUNCTION (**3h09min**).

Keep left, then take the track leading uphill to the right. This is a favourite take-off point for paragliders — you may envy them their mode of descent! The track fades away at a right-hand bend, and you will need to cross a barbed-wire fence and then climb the steep grassy bank to your left. The paint marks here are not easily seen, but once you find them the route is clear. At the top of the slope, follow the crest of the ridge up to your left. *(Note: On the descent it is easy to miss these marks. If other, confusing waymarks lead you to the bottom of this short ridge, look right, to locate the fence that you must cross to rejoin the correct route.)* The summit area is a collection of hillocks that would be very confusing in mist. The path leads you around and over several humps and dips before making the final short climb to the SUMMIT OF **Stol** (**4h06min**). A large mast and a rather ugly hut have spoilt the top, but they cannot detract from the marvellous views. The Julian Alps look close enough to touch, while in the opposite direction the plains of Italy seem to stretch to infinity. There is a visitors' book where you can record your achievement.

Return by your route of ascent to **Kobarid** (**7h20min**).

Left: Krn, the peak on the right (Walk 15) rises behind Sv. Anton and the charnel house in Kobarid (Walk 16). Do visit the museum, to learn more about Kobarid's history during World War I.

18 TOLMIN • ZABČE • KORITA ZADLAŠČICE • KORITA TOLMINKE • TOLMIN

Distance/time: 6.5km/4mi; 1h56min
Grade: easy; good paths and tracks, although rough in places and slippery if wet
Equipment: see page 38; walking shoes, torch advisable

How to get there: 🚌 or 🚐 to Tolmin. Park in the free car park near the church and Posta (post office), behind Slovenska Investicijska Banka.
Nearest accommodation: Tolmin

This is a real gem. Drama and beauty are combined in one small package where the *koritas* (gorges) of Zadlaščice and Tolminke meet. You will see a natural rock bridge, Dante's Cave and the impressive Hudičev Most (Devil's Bridge).

This walk sets out at the POST OFFICE in **Tolmin**. Walk in an easterly direction past the open-air market on the opposite side of the road and the BUS STATION on the left. Continue on the main road, ignoring any turn-offs left or right, to reach the bridge over the river **Tolminka** (8min). Immediately after the bridge, turn left beside a large chestnut tree onto a concrete path. The path joins a road just outside the village of **Zabče**. In the village, at a junction shaped like a tuning fork, take the left branch, and then keep left again at the next junction. You should then bear right at a fork, to go between a house and another building. After 100m you should pass two tall, narrow CONCRETE PILLARS that support a large vine next to an open barn — if you do not, you have missed the route! Just beyond these pillars a clear sign

indicates your path to the right, alongside an old STONE WALL (20min).

You soon leave the wall, bearing left along the top of a bank at the back of some houses. Go through a small METAL GATE and continue on a wider path beside a line of trees. A lovely vista opens out before you — undulating hay meadows dotted with barns and the wooded, cone-shaped hill of **Kozlov Rob** to the left. After another gate the path narrows and continues through woodland. Look out for a drinking point, a little SPRING piped up through a hollowed-out log — a simple but effective idea. You are now traversing a wooded hillside with wild flowers carpeting the sides of the path. A mossy water slide is crossed and after a few minutes the path begins to descend quite steeply to a SUSPENSION BRIDGE (42min) just above the confluence of the **Zadlaščica** and the **Tolminka** rivers — the hub of this walk.

Cross the bridge and turn right, steeply uphill, to a junction. Continue straight on along the path (well protected with a cable fence), above the steep sides of the **Korita Zadlaščice**. From the FIRST VIEWPOINT you look directly down into the gorge, but from the SECOND VIEWPOINT there is a

superb view up the gorge, to a
natural bridge formed by a huge
boulder called the '**Boar's Head**'
(photograph right). There is
another platform above the Boar's
Head (**53min**), but beyond that
the path is unprotected and
dangerous.

Return to the junction above the
suspension bridge and head uphill
to an asphalt road, where you turn
right to visit **Dante's Cave**
(**59min**). This cave, where the
writer spent some time in exile,
can only be explored a little way
without a torch.

Return down the road, and
continue on to **Hudičev Most**
(**1h03min**). This wide bridge
spans the gorge at a height of 60m
above the Tolminka and gives a
wonderful bird's-eye view of the
river. Pass through a short tunnel
and walk on down the road.

Near the bottom of the hill, take a
path off left; this doubles back
north, taking you down to the
river **Tolminka** and the
CONFLUENCE OF THE TWO GORGES
(**1h14min**). There are several
benches here; and it is a
marvellous setting (Picnic 7).
Cross the footbridge, meet a
junction and turn left. (A right
turn would take you back to the
bridge over the Zadlaščica in less
than two minutes).

This path, a wide, chiselled-out
ledge, takes you under the Devil's
Bridge and through a tunnel about
25m long (take great care here if
you do not have a torch). After a
rock arch the scene is spectacular.
The high cliffs of the narrow
Korita Tolminke are sculptured
and worn smooth by the river's
passage and the Tolminka is an
incredible translucent blue. The
path ends at a CAVE ENTRANCE
with a metal door (**1h17min**).

Now retrace your steps to the road
and turn left, to come to a bar.
Take the track behind the bar
(signposted to TOLMIN). It runs
through a field and passes between
a house and a little garden. Soon
you descend through the trees on a
cobbled path (look out for a tiny
grotto), to meet a road. Turn left,
passing a children's play area and a
WORLD WAR I CEMETERY. Continue
along the road, ignoring a road
merging from the right, and go by
a SAWMILL. Eventually, you will
come to a junction, where you
turn right along BAZOVIŠKA ULICA.
Carry straight on at another
junction, to where a flight of steps
leads down to the main road. Turn
right to reach the POST OFFICE in
Tolmin (**1h56min**).

See photograph pages 20-21
Distance/time: 18.5km/11.5mi; 8h04min
Grade: very strenuous, with total ascents of about 1400m/4600ft. This is a long and committing mountain ridge walk. Map and compass skills are essential, especially in poor weather.
Equipment: see page 38; walking boots, walking sticks

How to get there: 🚌 Take the narrow road 4.5km/2.75mi south-west of Podbrdo to Stržišče. Parking is limited, but a space may be found beyond the village and before the church or beyond the church on the track to Kal. *Please be considerate to the local villagers.*
Nearest accommodation: Most na Soči, Tolmin, Bohinjska Bistrica

This hike is superb, but it is only for the very fit and those accustomed to airy heights. After the initial ascent there follows a three-hour walk along an amazing ridge with breathtaking views.

Using the church **Sv. Ožbolt** just east of **Stržišče** as the **starting point**, follow the gravel track past a dilapidated old barn and a little SHRINE. In the tiny hamlet of **Kal** (**12min**), bear left and pass to the right of a WATER TROUGH, to find a grassy track leading away from the back of the houses. An easy climb through trees brings you to a junction at **Sedlo**, a col with a picnic table and bench (**42min**). Turn left on the clearly-marked path that begins a long ascent up through beautiful beech woods. The path zigzags either side of a ridge and you may be glad of the shade on a hot day. After 35 minutes of steady climbing you reach a CLEARING on the ridge where you can enjoy the view while sitting on a thoughtfully-provided log! In a further 15 minutes pass another VIEWPOINT called **Klopca** (**1h32min**) and not long after, you emerge from the trees onto the open hillside, where there is a MEMORIAL TO THE ALPINIST IVO SORLI (**1h36min**). The path now climbs a little more steeply before beginning a rising traverse across the hillside to a grassy col on the main ridge (**Čez Suho; 2h21min**). The view is staggering (and you may be as well!). The villages in Bohinj and

the lake can be seen below, but what holds the eye is Triglav and its neighbouring peaks. Turn left along the ridge and climb to DOM ZORKA JELINČIČA. Then scramble up a little path behind and to the left of the hut, to the SUMMIT OF **Črna Prst** (**2h40min**).
The walk continues west along the ridge, passing under the cables of a goods lift. After 10 minutes you reach a junction. Turn left off the ridge ('VOGEL' is painted on a rock) and begin the descent to another col, Vrata. This is the most difficult section of the walk, but there are secure cables. From **Vrata** (**3h05min**) the path climbs along the ridge, then traverses beneath the summit of **Četrt**.

From now on the path avoids all the summits along the ridge and there is surprisingly little extra climbing. It is a pure delight. Easy walking on the good path allows you to enjoy the extensive views. After passing the summits of **Konjski** and **Poljanski**, go around the grassy shoulder of **Matajurski Vrh**, where the terrain changes and becomes much more rocky. The way is still easy to follow and the path is clearly seen on the distant slopes, but now requires more care as you traverse the mountainside.

The path skirts under **Matajurski Vrh**, **Raskovec** and by **Suha Rodica**, which is an amazing mountain formed by leaning columns of rock. The final ridge to the **Rodica** summit again requires care, but on its grassy top you can rest and enjoy the incredible panoramas for one last time (**5h17min**). *But remember* that the descent, although easy, will take almost three hours.

You now descend in a south-westerly direction along a crest. After eight minutes, watch for a junction by some ruined walls, where you must turn left ('RUT' is painted on a rock). The path zigzags down gradually over stony ground and then through dwarf pine. It crosses several gullies on the open slopes before entering the trees and eventually reaching a track (**6h07min**).

Turn left downhill here. Ignore all side-tracks; follow the TARGET MARKS until you reach a SHARP HAIRPIN BEND to the right (**6h38min**), where a rough track climbs to the left. Take the wide grassy path below this track, where 'STRŽIŠČE' is written on a boulder.

The path traverses the side of a wooded ridge above Rut and, after 12 minutes, rounds the ridge and doubles back. This old route crosses several cascading streams and is falling away in places, so care is needed. At one point you cross a bridge with a decorated plaque dated 1933. Climb gently across the hillside until you reach a large CLEARING. The path, now wide and grassy, meets a track on the far side of this open area (**7h34min**).

Directly opposite is your descending path to Stržišče. It is a little over-grown just at the start, but there is a target mark on a tree. (*Do not* walk along the track to find it.) The rough and little-used path descends steeply through the trees and ends at a track behind a house. Continue on the track and then a concrete road to **Stržišče**. Turn left at the asphalt road and walk to **Sv. Ožbolt** (**8h04min**).

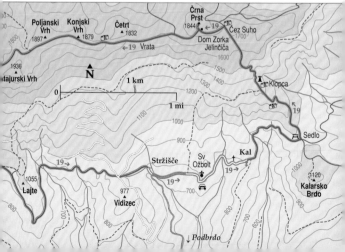

See also photograph in the box on page 21

Distance/time: 11.8km/7.3mi; 3h16min

Grade: easy; on good paths and tracks

Equipment: see page 38; walking shoes, swimsuit. Refreshments are available at Ukanc and Slap Savica.

How to get there and return: 🚗 or 🚌 to Ribčev Laz. Regular bus service from Bled calling at Ribčev Laz and Ukanc. To return catch the bus from the Hotel Zlatorog at Ukanc or see Alternative return on page 90.

Nearest accommodation: Ribčev Laz, Bohinjska Bistrica, Bled

Short walk: Ukanc — Slap Savica — Ukanc. 6km/3.8mi; 2h05min. Grade and equipment as main walk. Access: 🚗 Drive along the southern shore of Bohinjsko Jezero and park near the Hotel Zlatorog. 🚌 from Ribčev Laz to Hotel Zlatorog. From the hotel walk along the asphalt road, crossing the river, and join the main walk after approximately 10 minutes at the 1h23min-point. Continue on to Slap Savica and then return to Ukanc.

Enjoy a leisurely stroll along the north shore of Bohinjsko Jezero. There are ample opportunities for picnicking, and remember to take your swimsuit. Our walk includes Slap Savica, an amazing waterfall fed by the lakes in the Triglav Lakes Valley through an underground river.

Start at the ROAD BRIDGE ACROSS THE SAVA BOHINJKA in **Ribčev Laz**. On the far side, opposite the church of **Sv. Janez**, which has some superb 15th- and 16th-century frescoes, turn left along a gravel path above the shore of **Bohinjsko Jezero**. When you meet an asphalt road, follow it through the trees to a large CAR PARK. From here a track continues along the shore of the lake, passing gravel beaches and picnic spots (Picnic 9), to a green BARRIER (**15min**). Continue along the track and, just before entering thicker woodlands, you can look across the lake to the church of Sv. Duh on the southern shore with a fine backdrop of mountains. Eventually, beside a lovely beach, you pass a curious TREE STUMP that is now used as a SHRINE (**1h**).

Soon after, you cross a boulder-filled, dry river bed, and in a few minutes reach the western end of the lake at a grassy picnic area with a REFRESHMENT HUT (**1h15min**). Take a short path at the back of the hut to a gravel track, where you turn left. Follow this track to a T-junction at a small house (131 UKANC) on your left, and an old shed opposite (**1h23min**). Turn right, following the signs for SLAP SAVICA. In one minute you reach a junction just before a bridge. Bear right here, to cross another bridge after a few metres.

SLAP SAVICA is now clearly signposted. Look out for the decorated house with the Slovenian flag flying outside and a signpost indicating the distances to various capital cities — London 1200km! Stay on the main path, passing a WATER POINT and avoiding any minor turn-offs to the left or right. In a short while you will hear the roar of the fast-flowing **Savica River** below. Ignore a waymarked path heading up right into the trees (the route of Walk 21), and in two minutes you will cross a bridge spanning the wide boulder-strewn river and enter a car park by **Koča pri Savici** (**1h54min**). Go between a bar and a gift shop, to follow a path up to the kiosk where you must buy a ticket. From here, after crossing a stone bridge, the path winds steeply uphill for 20 minutes to eventually reach a shelter, the VIEWPOINT FOR **Slap Savica** (**2h14min**). This dramatic waterfall, shown overleaf, bursts from the cliffs at the rear of a rocky gully. You can get a little closer, but you may need a jacket! From here return to the junction beside 131 UKANC (the 1h23min-point in the outward walk; **3h02min**) and carry straight on, ignoring a turn to the right after

Bohinjsko Jezero

Left: monument to the first climbers of Triglav at Ribčev Laz; above: the dramatic burst of Slap Savica

three minutes. When you reach an asphalt road, follow it to the ZLATOROG HOTEL and BUS STOP in **Ukanc** (**3h16min**).

Alternative return (to Ribčev Laz) 5km/3m; 1h09min. From the ZLATOROG HOTEL continue along the road, past the ZLATOROG CAMPING SITE, to a crossroads. Turn left here and follow the roadside path. There are many areas where you can reach the lake on little paths through the trees. Along the way you pass the church of **Sv. Duh**, with its large mural of St. Christopher, before coming back to **Ribčev Laz**.

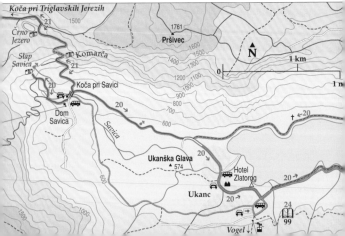

21 KOČA PRI SAVICI • ČRNO JEZERO • KOČA PRI SAVICI

Distance/time: 3.8km/2.3mi; 2h50min

Grade: Strenuous; a short, but exceptionally tough ascent of 641m/2102ft on a steep and sometimes exposed path. There are plenty of secure cables (one section requires a short traverse using metal pegs and a cable). ***Remember** that although the descent is not any more difficult, the feeling of exposure is **greatly increased**.*

Equipment: see page 38; walking boots, walking sticks

How to get there: 🚗 From Ribčev Laz drive along the southern shore of Bohinjsko Jezero, following signs for Slap Savica; park in the car park at the Koča pri Savici at the end of the road. 🚌 from Bled or Ribčev Laz to the Koča pri Savici.

Nearest accommodation: Ribčev Laz, Bohinjska Bistrica, Bled

Alternative walk: Triglav Lakes Valley. From Črno Jezero it is possible to continue along the Triglav Lakes Valley. The Koča pri Triglavskih Jezerih is a worthwhile and scenic objective. But it is a long walk (3h return from Črno Jezero), mostly through thick forest. If you would like to visit the valley, we suggest you stay in the hut overnight and explore this wonderful area in a more leisurely fashion. See page 38 for information about the Alpine Association and mountain huts.

Črno Jezero — the Black Lake

Climb the impossibly-steep and seemingly-impenetrable cliffs of Komarča to visit the lowest of the lakes in the Triglav Lakes Valley. This valley was created, so the story goes, by the rage of Zlatorog, the golden-horned Chamois (see box page 21). Črno Jezero is set amongst high cliffs and despite its name — Black Lake — it is hauntingly beautiful.

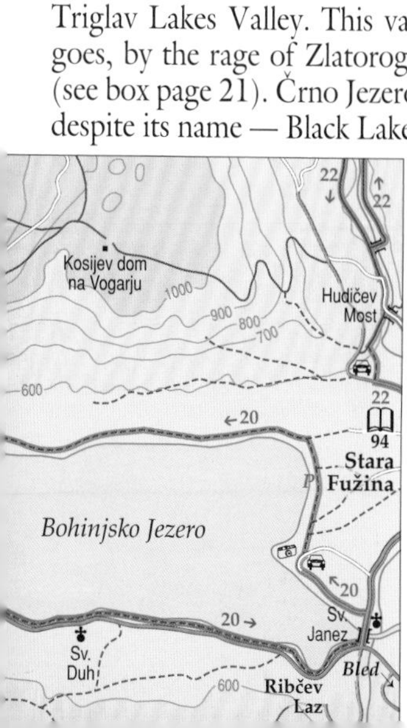

The walk starts at the **Koča pri Savici**. Take the path at the left of the *koča,* signposted 'ČRNO JEZERO 1-3/4HRS'. Cross the bridge and look up to the cliffs of Komarča. Believe it or not, this is where you are heading! At a junction (**2min**), turn left, still signposted 'ČRNO JEZERO', and climb easily through beech woods. Ignore a turning left (**15min**); continue up to another junction and keep right, following the 'KOMARČA' sign. The path now steepens and you find cable hand-rails just where you need them. Some 30 minutes from the last junction, a crag seems to bar the way. Skirt this to the right, soon enjoying splendid views back down to the valley. Seven minutes later you reach the trickiest part of the ascent. A short rock face, a few metres above a shallow gully, has to be crossed. Here the cable is more than a confidence booster — you *must* hang on to it and use the metal footholds too. Once across this obstacle, the path zigzags steeply uphill.

Eventually, you cross (easily) a narrow ridge of rock between the valley below and a deep gully. Notice the altitude of 1267m painted on a rock, and congratulate yourself on having scaled **Komarča (1h22min)**! Continue climbing, easily now, into the trees and enter a narrow defile that ends just above **Črno Jezero (1h31min)**. This is a most beautiful spot. The lake nestles in a rocky hollow surrounded by cliffs, larch trees and pines.
To return, retrace your steps to the **Koča pri Savici (2h50min)**.

22 STARA FUŽINA • MOSTNICA GORGE • VOJE • SLAP MOSTNICE • VOJE • MOSTNICA GORGE • STARA FUŽINA

See photograph opposite
Distance/time: 11.3km/7mi; 2h49min
Grade: easy; mainly on good paths and tracks
Equipment: see page 38; walking shoes. Refreshments are available at Slap Mostnice.
How to get there: 🚌 to Stara Fužina (limited parking). 🚐 from Bled to Ribčev Laz or (more infrequently) to Stara Fužina
Nearest accommodation: Ribčev Laz, Bohinjska Bistrica, Bled
Alternative start and end at Ribčev Laz: 13.3km/8.3mi;

3h31min. Start out by crossing the road bridge across the Sava Bohinjka in Ribčev Laz and follow this road to Stara Fužina, then pick up the main walk. To return, follow the route in the footnote on page 94.
Short Walk: Stara Fužina — Mostnica Gorge — Stara Fužina. 4.3km/2.7mi; 1h09min. Grade, equipment and access as main walk. Follow the main walk to the 32min-point. Cross the bridge and then turn left, following the main walk again from the 2h12min-point.

This low-level walk is full of variety. Starting from the pretty village of Stara Fužina, you soon reach the narrow and dramatic gorge shown opposite, cut by the Mostnica River and surrounded by lovely beech woods. Higher up the valley you walk through peaceful pastures to find Slap Mostnice (also known as Slap Voje), a gushing waterfall.

Starting from the BUS STOP and shops in **Stara Fužina**, walk towards the road bridge. Just before it, turn left along the road beside the river **Mostnica**. If Triglav is free of cloud, you will see the summit straight ahead. Cross the river and ignore two roads leading off to the right. Continue up the road past the RABIC INN and go through a METAL GATE. The asphalt soon ends, but a good track continues up to a stone bridge, **Hudičev Most** (**12min**), which spans the deep gorge. Cross the bridge and turn right, soon reaching your path, signposted to MOSTNICA KORITA. In five minutes you reach a 'TOBLERONE'-SHAPED HUT, covered in bark, where you turn right over another BRIDGE. Walk up the side of **Mostnica Gorge**, so deep and narrow in places that you cannot even see the river below. Take

care, as the edge is slippery. But the gorge is not continuous, and you follow the cascading river for a short while. Some rocks, sculptured by the water, make an ideal picnic spot above the sparkling pools of the river (one setting for Picnic 10).
Where a sign, 'SLONČEK', points to an unusual rock arch in the river bed, the second section of gorge begins. When you meet a track, turn left and cross the gorge on a wide BRIDGE (**32min**). Then turn right *(the Short walk turns left)* on a path that climbs above the gorge and is signposted 'VOJE'. Take care when walking on the tree roots, and follow the paint marks, ignoring any other paths, to reach a wide track (**44min**). Turn right, passing a small partisan MEMORIAL, before rounding a bend and coming to a hut (**Koča na Vojah**) and the Alpine valley of **Voje**.

Left: Mostnica Gorge (Walk 22)

93

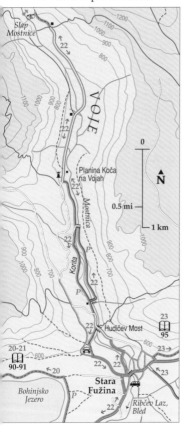

Slap Mostnice, at the head of Voje

Keeping on the main track, you come to a large HUT in 15 minutes. Continue straight on, following the sign for SLAP VOJE and, almost immediately, cross an old STONE BRIDGE over a small river. You now enter an area of grassland dotted with barns and cottages. Cows graze peacefully and the sound of their bells will accompany you on the next stage of the walk. This valley is flanked by steep wooded hillsides with the mountaintops just visible above. Eventually you come to an attractive CAFÉ/TEAROOM and four minutes later reach **Slap Mostnice** (**1h23min**). There is a path up to the base of the falls, but the spray may send you scurrying back!

To return, retrace your steps to the wide bridge at the 32min-point (**2h12min**). Do not cross it, but carry straight on, staying close to the side of the gorge. You soon cross a tributary on a little wooden FOOTBRIDGE. A little further on walk onto a narrow footbridge across the main gorge for an excellent view of the amazing sculptured rocks. But do not cross the gorge; return to continue the walk. You pass a few pleasant grassy areas (another setting for Picnic 10) close by the river, before returning to the HUT and the **Hudičev Most** (**2h31min**). Do not cross the bridge. Instead take a path that leads down a few wooden steps to the right. Follow this path for six minutes, to a CAR PARK, where you turn left down the road into **Stara Fužina**. At the junction in the village, bear left* to reach the main road and BUS STOP (**2h49min**).

*For the **Alternative end**, bear *right* at this junction and then immediately left, following the narrow street to meet the main road by a little shrine. Turn right here, to return to **Ribčev Laz**.

23 RIBČEV LAZ • RUDNICA • SREDNJA VAS • STUDOR • STARA FUŽINA • RIBČEV LAZ

See also photographs on pages 1, 20 (top), 21 (box), 36
Distance/time: 11.8km/7.3mi; 3h37min
Grade: moderate, with a climb of 400m/1300ft to Rudnica. Mainly on good paths and tracks, except for the steep and sometimes loose-surfaced descent from Rudnica
Equipment: see page 38; walking boots, walking sticks. Refreshments are available at Srednja Vas and Stara Fužina.
How to get there: 🚌 or 🚐 (from Bled) to Ribčev Laz
Nearest accommodation: Ribčev Laz, Bohinjska Bistrica, Bled
Alternative walk: Ribčev Laz — Brod — Srednja Vas — Studor — Stara Fužina — Ribčev Laz.
13.3km/8.3mi; 3h11min. Easy; equipment/access as main walk. Follow the main walk to the 11min-point, then continue round to the right, passing some guesthouses. Where the road ends beside a wooden shed, follow a track along the side of a field and keep left at a junction where you enter woodland. The track narrows; at a fork, keep right, to drop down to the river bank. After 20 minutes enter a field and head to the right

of the wooden shed on a faint track. Soon after, pass to the left of another shed ('Brod' is painted here). The track, now clearly defined, is easily followed towards Brod. It ends by some small gardens and stacks of logs, at an asphalt road. Do not cross the bridge to Savica, but carry on past the 'Brod' sign. Beyond a small farm, the road climbs to a fork. Take the left branch, still uphill (going downhill to the right would take you to the centre of the small village), to where the asphalt ends outside house No. 19. Fork left again, up into the trees. After 12 minutes you enter the high hay meadows; continue along the main track. Ignore two other tracks off left (the second one is signposted to Rudnica) and come to the next signposted junction. Turn left for 'Sr. Vas and Studor' and climb to a T-junction on a broad low ridge. Turn left here for 'Sr. Vas', heading directly towards the wooded hill of Rudnica. The path gently winds through the meadows to another junction, where you rejoin the main walk at the 2h05min-point. Now follow the main walk to the end.

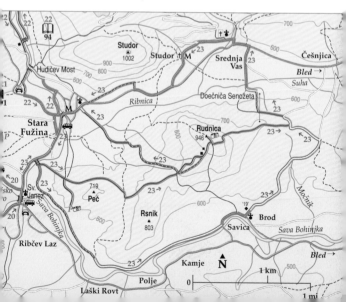

Short walk: Rudnica. 8.3km/ 5.2mi; 2h40min. Grade, equipment and access as main walk. Follow the main walk to Rudnica. From the summit retrace your steps to the hut in the highest pasture and walk to the refreshment hut. From here descend a steep, loose gravel track. After 15 minutes you enter a field with a hut to your left (you passed this hut on the opposite side on your ascent). Continue down the winding track, through two junctions. Ford a small stream at the bottom of the hill and cross a concrete bridge. The track continues to Stara Fužina, where you turn left and follow the main walk back to Ribčev Laz.

This walk explores the rural charms of the upper Bohinj Valley. You start with a pipe opener — climbing Rudnica, where you are rewarded with a bird's-eye view of the valley. Wandering through the beautiful hay meadows and fields of this landscape, you will see some of Slovenia's best-preserved *toplarji* and *kozolci* (see box page 36) and enjoy three lovely villages. There are other attractions, too — allow time to visit the museums at Studor and Stara Fužina.

Begin in **Ribčev Laz** by crossing the bridge over the **Sava Bohinjka**. If you can tear yourself away from this beautiful view of Lake Bohinj, continue along the road past **Sv. Janez**. Approximately 100m after the entrance sign for **Stara Fužina**, turn right over a wide CONCRETE BRIDGE (**11min**). Follow the track ahead, signposted to RUDNICA and PEČ, and after 10m take the path left into a field (clearly signposted). This path follows the edge of the field up into the trees. In a little CLEARING you come to a junction where the path to Peč heads off to the right (**22min**). This worthwhile detour

Hay barn (toplar) at Stara Fužina

(16min return) leads to a VIEW-POINT overlooking Ribčev Laz and Bohinjsko Jezero (Picnic 11). From the junction follow the sign to RUDNICA, and after six minutes come to a small wooden HUT in a clearing. Continue on the narrow path that crosses the clearing and, as you re-enter the woodland, take a slightly-overgrown path that contours the hillside (*do not* take the steep wide path that descends to the left). You soon come to small clearing and then another with a ruined HUT (with target marks and 'RUDNICA' written in red; **36min**). When you meet a junction, turn right uphill on the gravel track (signed 'RUDNICA'), but after about 120m fork left on a path (again signed 'RUDNICA'). This climbs quite steeply before levelling out by a large field with a HUT on your left (**1h06min**). Follow the edge of the pasture to the right, to meet a path that has climbed from Brod. Turn left uphill and soon enter a lovely old beech wood. The path follows the cliff-edge overlooking Brod and the lower valley. Leaving this wood, you enter the highest meadow, just above a REFRESH-

MENT HUT. Ahead is another HUT, where you meet a path climbing from the left. Join this to enter the wood, where TARGET MARKS lead you to a COLLECTION OF SIGNPOSTS and, 75m further on, a fine VIEW-POINT at the cliff edge (photograph page 20). Just behind it is the SUMMIT OF **Rudnica**, with a visitors' book and stamp (**1h31min**).

Return to the signposts and bear left towards BROD. The path is a little vague at first, but there are TARGET MARKS. Descend by the cliff edge for a short way, before dropping into a smooth-sided gully and following the sign to SREDNJA VAS. Take care to follow the target marks indicating the faint path that zigzags down the steep slope. The angle eases and you leave the woods, to enter a field. A track is seen ahead. Walk down beside the wood and then the fence, to meet this track. Turn left and come to a junction (**2h05min**; *the Alternative walk joins here*).

Turn left, crossing the hill, and enjoy the wonderful views of the high mountains above the villages and the patchwork of fields in the upper valley. Not far down the hill, on a long right-hand bend, fork left on a grassy track sign-posted 'SR. VAS'. Follow this under the ski tow, where a sign, 'SR. VAS', points you down a path beside a wooden fence — through a small wood and down to some hayracks beside a track. Nearby is the tiny ski station called **Doečniča Senožeta**. Turn left along the track; it bends right to cross a stream (just before a junction with a shrine). Carry straight on past some fine old hay barns, to reach the road at the edge of **Srednja Vas** (**2h25min**).

Turn left through this attractive village. The houses are bright with flowers, and some of the old buildings are decorated with farm implements and horse harness. After two minutes you reach the tiny square. A water trough, bench and table sit beneath a shady linden tree, just the place for a drink or an ice cream. Then walk around the corner on the right, and take the narrow road over a bridge, climbing the hill beneath the CHURCH (which is worth a visit, if just to see the beautiful graveyard). At the top of the hill, opposite the main entrance to the church, walk down the road that passes the GARNI PENSION. Just beyond the pension, turn right at a junction and walk a short way uphill. Then turn left downhill, still on an asphalt road. To your left are the craggy wooded slopes of Rudnica, while ahead the hill of Studor towers above the village of the same name. Soon you reach **Studor**, where the first house on the left is the **Oplen House Museum,** an old peasant cottage. Continue through the peaceful hamlet, keeping left by the SHRINE, to pass the Icelandic PONY RIDING CENTRE. After leaving the village walk down to the main road. Here you will see the traditional barns *(toplarji)*, some over 200 years old, which are often featured on postcards and in tourist brochures (**2h52min**; photograph page 36). Turn right, heading for STARA FUŽINA. Seven minutes later turn right on a short gravel track that heads towards the hill of Studor. Go through a wide gap in the hedge and turn left along this shady track, which ends at a gate near the CHURCH in **Stara Fužina**. Turn right along the road through the village and, at a fork, bear right downhill to a BRIDGE. Look out for **Planšarski Muzej** (the Alpine Dairy Museum). Pass the bus stop, bar and shops and continue on the main road back to **Ribčev Laz** (**3h37min**).

24 SKI HOTEL VOGEL • PLANINA ZADNJI VOGEL • VOGEL • ŠIJA • SKI HOTEL VOGEL

Distance/time: 10km/6.2mi; 3h40min

Grade: strenuous, with a total ascent of approximately 600m/ 2000ft. A high-level mountain walk on waymarked paths, involving some easy scrambling. Vogel is liable to lightning strikes; avoid if storms are forecast!

Equipment: see page 38; walking boots, walking sticks

How to get there: cable car to the Ski Hotel (see local tourist information centres for timetable and current price). 🚌 From Ribčev Laz drive along the southern shore of Bohinjsko Jezero; follow signs for the Ski Hotel and cable car (see map pages 90-91). 🚐 from Bled or Ribčev Laz to the cable car.

Nearest accommodation: Ribčev Laz, Bohinjska Bistrica, Bled

Y ou may not consider yourself a mountain walker, but *do* take the cable car to the Ski Hotel and enjoy the incredible views over Bohinjsko Jezero and to Triglav and the Julian Alps. However, the effort of climbing to the summit of a mountain is always rewarded, and Vogel will not disappoint you!

Starting out from the UPPER CABLE CAR STATION, walk past the SKI HOTEL (Picnic 12) and continue along the wide gravel track until you meet a junction on a bend. Although this walk is a mountain climb, it starts with a descent, so turn right downhill and follow the signs to ZADNJI VOGEL. The track, through mixed woodland, only loses a little height. Ignore turns to the left and right; after 15 minutes, as you walk under a chair lift, you can see Vogel directly ahead. At **Planina Zadnji Vogel** (**20min**), walk between the buildings and past a large wooden water trough. Bear right here to reach a BOULDER on which various

destinations are painted (we disagree with the times!). Turn left uphill for Vogel on a narrow path that leads to a shallow, grassy valley on the hillside. The path climbs through the centre of this hollow, to a boulder where 'VOGEL' is indicated to the right. In eight minutes, at a crossroads where 'VOGEL' is again painted on a boulder (**55min**), keep straight on. Just around the bend you will see Vogel again, the middle of the three summits.

The path now climbs gradually along the left-hand side of a high, rocky valley. A few metres after passing a turn to your left (where the walk continues on your

View eastwards to Rodica from the summit of Vogel

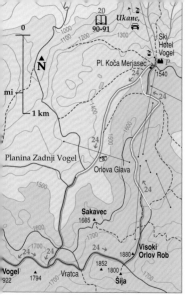

climb. It looks much worse than it is, the first few feet being the hardest. There are paint marks to follow and you will only occasionally need your hands. At the top, the path continues by traversing the hillside, passing through patches of dwarf pine. Ahead is the summit of Šija. When you meet the MAIN RIDGE CREST again, climb along it for a few meters, before turning left and traversing gently uphill. The path edges around the side of two large craters before contouring underneath the summit of Šija to a crossroads. Turn right if you want to climb the short distance to the summit of Šija, or turn left to continue. The path descends for a short way, then climbs a little hillock, to the right of its summit, to reach the HIGHEST CHAIRLIFT (**2h52min**).

The descent from here is easy but can be a little confusing, as paths and tracks go off in all directions. Your first objective is the bottom of this chairlift. Two high fences guide you down a steep, loose slope. When the descent eases, look for a signpost on your left indicating a path to the ZADNJI VOGEL CHAIRLIFT. Follow this, in one minute passing a boulder marked 'SKI HOTEL'. This path goes through an area of mini craters and dwarf pine, to end at a wide gravel track, which you follow up a short steep slope. Walk under the chairlift and continue on to **Orlova Glava**, a flat area where many chairlifts and tows converge (**3h16min**). From the left of another chairlift (the middle one you could see when descending to Orlova Glava) a track now descends. Follow this to the bottom of the chairlift. From here take a path around the edge of a hollow, back to the SKI HOTEL and CABLE CAR STATION (**3h40min**).

return), you reach the CREST OF THE MAIN RIDGE (**1h03min**). Before you are the wooded hills of the Karst plateau around Cerkno and Idrija, which stretch out into the distance. Follow the path up the ridge to your right for about 100m, before traversing the hillside to meet the crest again (**1h16min**). Ahead is a short, easy scramble, but it requires surefootedness and a head for heights. When the ridge becomes too steep the path traverses again, this time over a long open slope. At the far side, take a paint-signed path that climbs directly up to the crest. You must now double back, turning left to walk along the ridge to reach the SUMMIT OF **Vogel** (**1h46min**). The views are extensive and include the Adriatic Sea off Italy while, in the opposite direction, Triglav and his subordinates dominate the scene. Do not forget to sign the book! To return, retrace your steps to the 1h03min-point, at the top of the rocky valley (**2h16min**). A short way down, take the path to the right that hugs the bottom of the cliffs and leads to the base of a steep wide gully, which you must

See photographs page 23
Distance/time: 6km/3.7mi;
1h26min
Grade: easy; on good paths
throughout

Equipment: see page 38; walking
shoes
How to get there: 🚌 or 🚍 to
Idrija
Nearest accommodation: Idrija

If you are having a busy cultural day in Idrija learning about mercury-mining and lace-making, take time out to enjoy this peaceful stroll along the *rake* (water channel) to one of Slovenia's most important natural phenomena — the wild lake, Divje Jezero. Along the way you can visit the *kamst*, the largest wooden waterwheel (13.6m in diameter) ever built in Europe. It powered the pumps that drained the mercury mines and ran uninterrupted for 158 years until 1948.

Start the walk from the rear of the BUS STATION in **Idrija**, where an asphalt road climbs the hill. When the road divides (**4min**), fork left and continue to an INFORMATION BOARD (**9min**). To your left a short path leads downhill to the *kamst*. To your right is a large building with 'Srečno' (Good Luck) written on it in large letters and, to its left, a mine tunnel dated 1898. The way forward is through the building ahead, under a covered passageway between metal cages. Here are the old trains that worked in the mine.

On the far side of the passageway you meet the *rake* that powered the waterwheel. You will follow this for most of the walk. Occasionally it passes through a tunnel or goes underneath the wide, easy path, but mainly you walk beside it through beech woods. Below and to your left is the river **Idrijca**.

Eventually (**30min**) you will notice a NEW ROAD BRIDGE on the far side of the river. This is your signal to look for a split in the fencing (there is a faint arrow on a tree), where your ongoing path doubles back to cross a SUSPENSION BRIDGE. (If you miss this turning you will reach a dam across the river. Retrace your steps for two minutes to find the path.) Cross the bridge and turn left down the road, coming to a CAR PARK in about 100m. There are some INFORMATION BOARDS here, but only one is in English. Opposite there are some stone steps. Climb these and follow the path that circles **Divje Jezero** (**43min**).

It may seem an idyllic aquamarine pool, but Divje Jezero has a savage appetite — having claimed the lives of men who tried to explore its source, which is more than 80m beneath the usually-quiet surface. After heavy rain the pool seems to 'boil', as water bubbles furiously from the hidden spring. Return to **Idrija** the same way (**1h26min**).

26 SLAP PRŠJAK

See photograph page 24
Distance/time: 2.5km/1.6mi;
1h05min
Grade: easy, but on narrow paths,
sometimes above steep drops
Equipment: see page 38; walking
boots
How to get there: 🚗 Drive about
29km/18mi northwest of Idrija or
11km/6.8mi southeast of Most na
Soči and cross the river Idrijca at
Dolenja Trebuša, signposted to
Čepovan and Vojsko. Bear right
through Dolenja Trebuša and pass
the church. At a junction, fork left
along a narrow road (signposted
to Idrija), to a bar (5.5km/3.4m

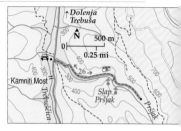

from the main road). Park here
(you cannot miss this bar, because
a waterfall is painted on the
exterior).
Nearest accommodation: Idrija,
Tolmin

Slovenia has many unspoilt hidden gems, and on this short
walk you visit beautiful waterfalls well away from the main
tourist routes. Slap Pršjak is ideal for a relaxing day or a leg
stretcher when you are touring.

Start out at the BAR: walk up the
path behind the parking area on
the right-hand side of the **Pršjak**
stream, quickly passing a saw
bench. A log across the path has
'SLAP' written on it (**2min**). Cross
the stream here on a small stone
and concrete walkway, and turn
right on the other side.
You now gradually climb alongside, and then above the stream on
an excellent, well-graded path
through the woods. Cross a very
small stream, with a drinking cup
provided in case you are thirsty, to
reach a VIEWPOINT overlooking the
waterfalls of **Slap Pršjak** (**20min**).
The upper fall drops into a little
heart-shaped pool and the lower,
but much longer one, cascades like
a mare's tail into a large pool. The
latter is a favourite spot for the
adventurous. They are lowered
down the fall on a rope and then,
with about 6m to go, are released
to plummet into the deep ice-cold
water!
Continue on the path that now
traverses above steep slopes. The
path is good, but narrow. Just

after entering the woods again, a
little path descends to the stream
between the two falls. Make a
small diversion here if you would
like a closer look at this exquisite
miniature waterfall. It is steep and
a little slippery at the bottom, but
you can get a good view before
you reach this section.
Unfortunately, there are not many
comfortable or safe places to
picnic while viewing the falls. So
continue along the main path,
above a series of small cascades, to
reach a small CLEARING with a
ruined building in the centre
(**36min**). Here you can bask in the
sun or enjoy the shade of the
surrounding trees in a secluded
setting.
The path does continue upwards
to some old houses that are
occasionally occupied, but we
recommend that you turn back
here, to the BAR (**1h05min**).
Note: The bridge painted on the
bar wall — **Kamniti Most** — is
just four minutes' walk up the
road.

27 PREDMEJA • KOČA A. BAVČERJA • KUCELJ • KOČA A. BAVČERJA • PREDMEJA

Distance/time: 9.8km/6mi; 3h16min

Grade: moderate, with a steep initial climb of 320m/1050ft. Mainly on good paths and tracks

Equipment: see page 38; walking boots, walking sticks. In season, refreshments are available from the mountain hut (Koča A. Bavčerja).

How to get there: 🚗 Follow Car Tour 2 or, direct from Idrija, drive 11km/6.9mi southeast to Gudovič then turn left to Col (16km/10mi). Turn right to reach Predmeja in a further 15km/9.4mi and park at the T-junction where a right turn leads to Lovke (see Short walk).

Nearest accommodation: Idrija, Nova Gorica

Short walk: Koča A. Bavčerja — Kucelj — Koča A. Bavčerja. 4.5km/2.8mi; 1h26min. Easy. Equipment: walking shoes. Access: Drive (as opposite) to Predmeja, and turn right towards Lovke. After 2.8km/1.7mi turn left on a well-surfaced forestry track. Ignore a right turn and park at the Koča A. Bavčerja after 4km/2.5mi. Follow the main walk from the 1h-point to Kucelj and then back to the mountain hut.

Enjoy the magnificent beech woods of this limestone escarpment that overlooks the Vipava Valley. The vineyards and hill villages have a distinct Italian flavour, and Kucelj gives you a bird's-eye view of the scene.

Begin the walk at the T-JUNCTION in **Predmeja**: climb the stone steps up to the PICNIC TABLES on the grassy bank next to the junction. Then head left on a path into the trees, clearly signposted to KOČA A. BAVČERJA. Soon a well-waymarked path joins from the left and you follow this uphill, at first through pine and then predominantly beech woods. Climb over the top end of an OLD WALL (**22min**), and two minutes later reach a very large picnic table and VIEWPOINT. Continue uphill, soon coming to an area of large boulders and rocky outcrops, after which you climb more steeply to join a FOREST ROAD (**45min**). Turn left along this road, firstly on a gravel and then on an asphalt surface, and follow it uphill. There is a picnic table with lovely views at the highest point. The road reverts to gravel and heads slightly downhill to reach KOČA A. BAVČERJA (**1h**). From the far side of the mountain hut follow the path signposted to KUCELJ downhill, through a metal BARRIER and alongside a small line of trees. Keep the field on your

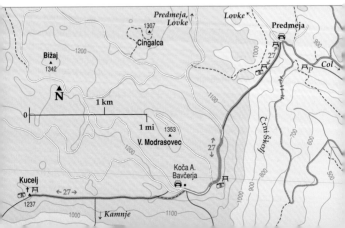

On the summit of Kucelj; notice the clear target mark on the boulder in the foreground.

left. The route is well waymarked and quickly takes you into woodland and through a limestone outcrop. The clearing beyond opens up more views of the valley. Continue down through pine trees, ignoring a path left to Kamnje. A little further on, keep straight ahead at a crossroads, where Kamnje is again signposted to the left (**1h15min**).

In a rough grassy clearing you can see your objective ahead above the trees. At first the climb is gentle but, after a left turn, the path steepens and emerges from the trees at the edge of the escarpment. Walk through a few dwarf pines and then follow an old, low drystone wall uphill through limestone boulders and spiky outcrops. The going is easy as the path follows a grassy ridge, covered in wild flowers and dotted with the occasional pine tree. The final climb to the SUMMIT OF **Kucelj** (**1h43min**) is simple, and you are rewarded with fantastic views all around. Glimpsed above the wooded hills to the north are the Julian Alps, but the fertile Vipava Valley far below to the south is fascinating. The scene is laid out like a map, and the villages and vineyards are easily picked out. On the summit itself there is a picnic table, a metal cross, the customary visitors' book … and a curious wooden mushroom. Kucelj is a haven for paragliders, and if the wind conditions are right you may see them as they ride the updraft that sweeps up the escarpment.

To return, retrace your steps to **Predmeja** (**3h16min**).

28 HRASTOVLJE • SV. ŠTEFAN • DOL • V. GRADEŽ • LAČNA • HRASTOVLJE

See also photograph page 26
Distance/time: 10.5km/6.6mi; 3h14min
Grade: easy-moderate; mainly on good paths and tracks
Equipment: see page 38; walking boots, walking sticks
How to get there: See Car tour 3, page 26, and park in the lay-by near the church of Sv. Trojica.
Nearest accommodation: any of the coastal resorts
Short walk: Hrastovlje — Sv. Štefan — Dol — Hrastovlje.

4km/2.5mi; 1h03min. Easy; equipment and access as main walk. Follow the main walk to Dol (the 46min-point). Turn right and follow the road to leave the small village, going through a huge and impressive stone-built railway embankment. Continue past an unusual commemorative stone, celebrating the 500th anniversary of the frescoes in Hrastovlje's church. Just beyond this you pass a shrine at a junction where you turn right and return to your car.

I n this walk we explore the fringe of the Karst plateau that rears up just inland from Slovenia's short coastline. Hrastovlje is the home of Sv. Trojica, a plain and unassuming little church on the outside but which houses some truly amazing 15th-century frescoes within its tiny interior. If you are looking for an antidote to the busy coastal resorts and roads, then this peaceful area is ideal.

Set out from the little parking area near **Sv. Trojica** on the edge of **Hrastovlje** (Picnic 15). Following clear waymarking, walk up towards the church and take the first turn to the left, down into the village. Ignore a turn to the left and soon reach the main village road. Turn right here, to go downhill and pass HOUSE NO. 24. Turn right at the next junction and then right again, down towards the bottom of the valley.

After the last house on your left the asphalt road becomes a gravel track and descends to an ELEC-TRICITY BUILDING (**8min**). Turn right here, still downhill, cross a little BRIDGE and then head left uphill. The track becomes much rougher as it climbs past olive trees and vines. At the top of a rise, with vines on your left, take the steep path to the right that climbs up to the RAILWAY LINE. Cross this *with care* and continue steeply uphill, following the waymarks over the rocky ground. At the top you reach a gravel track opposite a

small partisan MEMORIAL (**24min**). There are lovely views back across the valley to Hrastovlje from here and to your left is the tiny church of **Sv. Štefan**.

There are *no waymarks* on the next section of the walk. Turn right along the track, and you will notice that there is a railway on both sides. These are not separate lines; the railway makes a tight turn in a tunnel behind Dol. You reach **Dol** in 16 minutes, by the large *gasilski dom* (fire station). Descend from here towards the houses, ignoring a narrow road coming in on the right, and walk below the plain-looking CHURCH. At a junction (**46min**) keep straight on. *(But for the Short walk turn right here.)* You pass an old WATER PUMP and trough and immediately bear left between a wall and a building.

One minute later the asphalt gives way to a gravel surface. Ignore a track off to the right that heads into a field and continue to a BRIDGE ACROSS THE RAILWAY LINE.

The fortified walls of Sv. Trojica and the frescoed interior of this beautiful church (below). See also page 26.

Cross this and keep on the now-rougher track, up through shrubby trees (where you may see the odd waymark). About 18 minutes from the bridge ignore a track off to the right and, six minutes later, ignore another track heading left into the trees. Continue climbing; in a further five minutes you leave

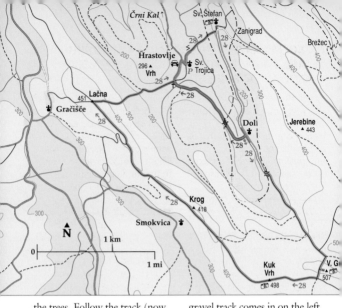

the trees. Follow the track (now clearly waymarked) as it bends to the right and makes the final short climb to the top of the grassy hill. At the track's highest point the SUMMIT OF V. Gradež is 50m to your left (**1h36min**). From this rather flat-topped hill there are fine views all around, especially along the escarpments that mark the edge of the Karst and across to nearby Croatia.

Continue along the grassy track for two minutes to a crossroads, and turn right along a clear track signposted to LAČNA. In another two minutes, at the end of a little wall, keep left on the main track. In a further six minutes you reach a SIGNPOST (where the flat top of **Kuk Vrh** is marked by a pole about 200m away). From the sign the track runs straight ahead for 40m, then turns right. You can now see the next stage of your walk all the way to Lačna. Follow the easy track down along the ridge, through scattered trees. You pass the top of **Krog** — just a bump on the ridge — and look down right over Sv. Štefan, nestling at the foot of the escarpment that stretches all the way to Črni Kal. As you start to climb Lačna a

gravel track comes in on the left (**2h16min**). Ignore this and walk past large heaps of stones that are of archaeological interest, to continue along the track. After 15 minutes you must find a little path that goes right. It starts a few metres in front of a DRYSTONE WALL, just where the track begins a gentle descent. Follow this way-marked path over a collapsed section of the wall to a junction at the SUMMIT OF Lačna (**2h36min**). Hrastovlje is clearly signposted, so cross the wall again and follow the narrow path as it descends the wooded slopes of Lačna.

The path crosses stable scree slopes, from where there are fine views down across the vines to the village and church, and then descends (sometimes steeply on a slippery surface) to a wide level path. Turn left here and, in one minute, turn right downhill. You now cross abandoned terraces and emerge from the trees at the edge of the vineyards. Follow the farm track downhill from here to a motorable track (**3h08min**). Turn right, in five minutes reaching the asphalt road by a BAR and a SHRINE. Bear left, quickly regaining **Sv. Trojica** (**3h14min**).

106

29 ŠKOCJAN CAVES VISITOR CENTRE • GRAD ŠKOLJ • FAMLJE • GRAD ŠKOLJ • ŠKOCJAN • MATAVUN • ŠKOCJAN CAVES VISITOR CENTRE

See photograph page 25
Distance/time: 10.8km/6.7mi; 2h40min
Grade: easy-moderate; mainly on good paths and tracks
Equipment: see page 38; walking boots, walking sticks, swimsuit
How to get there: 🚌 to the Škocjan Caves Visitor Centre
Nearest accommodation: Lipica, Postojna
Short walks (grade and access as main walk; walking shoes will suffice)

1 Naravni Most. 1.8km/1.1mi; 27min. Follow the main walk for about 15 minutes and take the right turn, which leads to the natural bridge (Naravni Most). Climb up to Matavun and then turn right, following the main walk from the water hole.
2 Škocjan circuit. 2.3km/ 1.4mi; 29min. Follow the main walk to the 19min-point. Bear right and walk up to the church in Škocjan. Then follow the main walk from the 2h33min-point.

A fter you have visited the Škocjan Caves and learned more about this UNESCO World Heritage site, why not explore further upstream along the river bank and out in the open air? Our walk takes you around the rim of one of the huge collapsed caves and then down to the gently-flowing Reka. You will visit castle ruins standing above a deep gorge and perhaps bathe in one of the lovely river pools.

The walk begins at the **Škocjan Caves Visitor Centre**. Pass the ticket office, shop and restaurant, to leave the complex through an automatic glass door. Go down the steps ahead and after the first flight, turn left along a wide path to a VIEWPOINT (**6min;** photograph page 25).
Continue along the path for another five minutes, to a junction. Turn sharp right, following the CHURCH SYMBOL. The path skirts the edge of some high cliffs (Picnic 16a) and descends to another junction opposite a small field (Picnic 16b). (*Short walk 1 goes*

right here.) Carry straight on, climbing a little, to pass the setting for Picnic 16c. Then you join an asphalt road beside some houses. Where the road bears right up to Škocjan church, turn left down a track (**19min**). (*But for Short walk 2, bear right.*) Follow the track to the valley floor, where you meet another junction; turn sharp right here, on a waymarked track. In four minutes ignore a track going downhill to the left. You are now walking to the left of an old walled-in pasture, and soon you will hear the river **Reka** ahead. The track ends at an old RUINED MILL, from where a path continues. The wide, slowly-flowing river is popular in summer, and soon you come to a volleyball court and diving board. Three minutes

107

beyond the mill ruins, the path divides and you must climb to the left. (The start of this path is a little overgrown; if you come to a large broken wall that crosses the river, you have missed it! Retrace your steps for 40m.) The waymarked path climbs a little and then continues along an attractive, wide rocky shelf above the river where it flows through a cliff-bounded gorge. You soon drop again to walk beside the river for a short distance. Cliffs then bar the way once more, and the path has to climb, this time steeply, to the rim of the gorge. Near the top there is a superb VIEWPOINT, where you can see down the valley and back to the church at Škocjan. At the top, turn right along the edge of a field and beside the rim of the gorge to reach a large ruined and overgrown castle, **Grad Školj (53min)**. Unfortunately the gates are locked. Turn left along a good track, but after only 50m, take a waymarked path that descends to the right. This is a steep and some-times slippery way back down to the river. At the base of the nearby cliffs, look out for some strange stalactite-like columns. Continue along the river bank, eventually passing through a small orchard and reaching a cobbled track that leads to a MODERN HOUSE (**1h17min**). Take the track to the right, and in two minutes keep right at another junction, to the ROAD BRIDGE across the Reka (**1h21min**). The bridge, high above the deep and placid river, has a diving board. On the far side, take a little path that starts by an INFORMATION BOARD and leads in 100m or so to a rocky eyrie. This is a quiet vantage point for a refreshing break.

To return, retrace your steps to the MODERN HOUSE (the 1h17min-point) and follow the track around it and up to **Famlje**. This is a peaceful little place with beautiful flower gardens and old vines. Our walk follows the cycle route through the village. Keep left at the first junction, and then left again, climbing uphill past house No. 21 to another junction (**1h33min**). Turn sharp left behind No. 21 and follow the narrow asphalt road above the fields and into the trees. In three minutes, where the road bends right, continue straight ahead on a good track (still the cycle route). Keep on this old, well-defined way, to reach a junction after 12 minutes. Here you leave the cycle route, turning left along a fainter track that leads back to **Grad Školj**. The approach, probably the original entrance, is along a stone-built embankment (**1h51min**). You now retrace your steps back to the junction at the edge of Škocjan village (the 19min-point of the outward route). Turn left here and walk up the road, turning left again to pass an old WELL and visit the CHURCH (**2h33min**). Above the door is the date 1607 and the church has, unusually, a separate bell tower. At the rear there is a fine viewpoint looking back down the valley.

Return to the road through the houses and turn left. Look for a METAL GRID set in the wall on your left, and peer down into the depths of the forbidding **Ukroglica**, another collapsed cave. Almost immediately, bear right on a sign-posted path beside the small, thatched MUSEUM. Follow the wall-lined path to **Matavun**. At a track just opposite a bar, turn left and immediately cross the asphalt road, to walk behind an artificial WATER HOLE (*Short walk 1 rejoins here*). Turn right along a track for 80m, then climb steps back up to the **Visitor Centre (2h40min)**.

See also photograph page 29
Distance/time: 9km/5.6mi;
2h23min
Grade: easy-moderate. On good
tracks and paths, with a climb of
539m/1768ft
Equipment: see page 38;

walking boots. Refreshments are
available from Dom Slivnica.
How to get there: 🚗 to
Cerknica; park near the town
centre. Or 🚐 from Postojna
Nearest accommodation:
Postojna

Cerknica is famous for its nearby 'disappearing lake', and
Slivnica is a superb vantage point from which to view the
immensity of this natural phenomenon, shown on page 29.
Depending on the time of year that you visit this area, you
may see hay-making in progress on the dry bed of the lake or
fishermen in boats enjoying their sport. After the initial climb,
Slivnica offers an easy stroll across green pastures with the lure
of a refreshing drink at the *dom*.

Start the walk from the POST
OFFICE in Cerknica. Walk southeast in the direction of Snežnik
(signposted), passing the TOURIST
INFORMATION CENTRE and crossing
the bridge over the river
Cerkniščica. Pass the Živila
Supermarket and the Kekec Bar,
then turn left at the next junction.
There is a sign here, 'DOM
SLIVNICA 1.5HRS'.
Turn right in 50m, up a wide
asphalt road. Ignore a turn off to
the right and keep straight ahead
at a crossroads. You can see the
summit of Slivnica ahead as you

pass through 'suburban' Slovenia.
Ignore the next turn to the left and
follow the road as it climbs up and
to the left towards the trees.
Where the asphalt ends (12min),
turn right up a gravel track that
soon becomes a path as you enter
the trees. The path is easy to
follow, but is *not* waymarked.
After five minutes you come to a
gravel road: cross it, then take the
left-hand path on the far side.
Continue climbing through
shrubby trees; in another seven
minutes you reach a wide, well-
used path (25min), where you

Approaching the summit of Slivnica

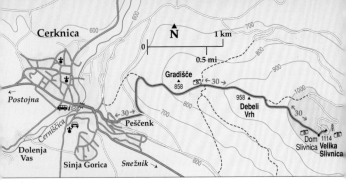

Wedding carriage at Snežnik Castle (Picnic 18), easily reached from Cerknica (Car tour 4)

turn right. *Keep this junction in mind*: it is easy to miss on the descent.*

In a further four minutes you meet another path, wider still, where you turn right again and continue steadily uphill. You may now see the occasional waymark. After nine minutes you emerge from the trees, to see the *dom* and the summit ahead and enjoy your first views south over the 'disappearing lake', Cerkniško Jezero. You are now on the CREST OF THE RIDGE. Where the path divides, take the right-hand option, soon climbing a STILE over a fence. The ridge crest is broad, with a steady climb to a grassy summit called **Debeli Vrh (55min)**. To the southeast is Snežnik, the highest non-Alpine mountain in Slovenia, dominating the lower hills of this region. Continue along the ridge through

lush pastures that are dotted with trees; beyond a STILE the path makes its last climb up to the *dom*. DOM SLIVNICA (**1h11min**) offers welcome refreshments, but you are not at the summit yet! You can make your way up through the trees to the left of the *dom* to an upper car park, from where a waymarked path leads to the SUMMIT OF **Slivnica** (**1h17min**). (Alternatively, you can make your way to the upper car park by following the gravel road to the left, and then turn right at the first junction.) Unfortunately, the bristle of masts quite spoil the summit itself, and trees obscure some of the views. However, you can see clearly to the distant hills and mountains in the north and northwest. Do not forget to sign the book!

Stop at the *dom* to enjoy the views over the lake before you retrace your steps back to **Cerknica** (**2h23min**).

---

*If you miss this junction on the descent, you will meet the gravel road. Cross this and follow a path which emerges from the trees onto an open ride. Follow this downhill and work your way through a

maze of paths, keeping to the right of the suburban houses, to join a road. Turn left, quickly reaching the main road and your route of ascent.

31 RAKOV ŠKOCJAN

Distance/time: 5km/3mi; 1h26min

Grade: easy, but note that after heavy rain parts of the walk may be inaccessible due to flooding.

Equipment: see page 38; walking shoes. Refreshments are available in season from the Hotel Rakov Škocjan.

How to get there: 🚗 From Postojna follow Car tour 4. Just after the 4km sign on the 914 road, turn right along the unsurfaced rock road. Drive over a natural rock bridge (Veliki Naravni Most) and past the hotel. Just after the 3.5km post, ignore a turn to the left. The parking area, where the walk starts, is 100m further along the road. If driving from Cerknica,

turn left about 3km north of Cerknica. Follow the unsurfaced road and signs to Rakov Škocjan.

Nearest accommodation: Postojna

Optional cave exploration: Moderate-strenuous. Equipment: walking boots, walking sticks and torch

We make no excuses for writing up this nature trail, even though it is waymarked (red/blue) and there is an excellent booklet about it available from the tourist information centre in Cerknica. Over the centuries ancient limestone deposits have been raised above sea level, and the action of weathering and rain have produced the amazing Karst features of sinkholes, disappearing rivers, vast cave systems and collapsed caves such as those at Škocjan (Walk 29). Here, at Rakov Škocjan, there is much on offer in a short easy circuit — a river emerging from, and then disappearing into, underground caverns, wonderful natural rock bridges and more. There are many quiet picnic areas and plenty of shade for hot days. This walk will not wear you out, but will give you much to photograph and remember.

Start out at the CAR PARK for **Rakov Škocjan**. Walk along a path on the opposite side of the road from the car parking area. A signpost shows the way and quickly leads to a small picnic area. From the right of the tables, a path leads to a natural rock bridge, the **Mali Naravni Most** (**2min**). You can see down into the collapsed caves (**Zelške Jame**) and walk over the narrow bridge itself. Here you find BOARD NO. 1 and the START OF THE NATURE TRAIL. (Optional: You can explore Zelške Jame when the river is dry or low:

from the viewpoint, look for a path behind you which descends into one of the collapsed caves and the river Rak. It is not difficult but it can be slippery. A torch is not necessary here, but you *will* need one to explore some of the smaller caves. A causeway takes you through a natural tunnel, after which you cross the river on a little stone bridge. The path continues through another tunnel, again on a causeway, to enter an amazing amphitheatre. It is wonderful! From this collapsed cave you can look up to the rock

111

bridge and where you were standing only a few minutes ago. Return by retracing your steps.) The main walk returns from Board No 1 to the picnic area, from where you follow a path that starts to the right of the information board and descends to an unsurfaced road. Cross the road to BOARD NO. 2 (**5min**).

Another two minutes brings you to BOARD NO. 3 and the **Rak Spring**, a cave entrance from where the river Rak emerges. (You can descend a slippery gully behind the board for a closer look and to see the ruins of a water-powered sawmill.)

To continue, follow the narrow path that climbs up through the rocks, to the right and behind this board. (Do *not* take the obvious path that heads to the right — it is the wrong way.) You soon get another view of Rak Spring as you descend towards the river. Carry on along the woodland path to BOARD NO. 4, which is 20m to the left of the path and beside a grassy clearing. Continue along beside

Zelške Jame: on the second causeway leading to the amphitheatre

the river, to reach a grassy field with electricity poles running through it. There is a waymark on the first pole. Turn right up to the second pole, and then turn left to find the waymarked route again and, very soon, BOARD NO. 5. Ten metres beyond the board, turn left downhill and cross a FOOTBRIDGE over the river (**20min**).

On the far side there is a waymarked path that scrambles up through the rocks on your left to the Hotel Rakov Škocjan. But an easier way to continue the walk (or go to the hotel) is to follow the *unmarked* path along the bank of the river. Where the path begins to climb to the left and up to the hotel, head *right* between some rocks. You will soon find the waymarks again and, after crossing a small footbridge, you reach BOARD NO. 6.

The path continues, passing BOARDS NO. 7 AND 8A, where you can see water bubbling out as a spring from under some rocks. Head up to the road, which is just above, and turn right. After 10m turn left to cross the road into the trees once more. The path leads to **Kotel**, another spring, and BOARD 8B. Turn right here; you soon recross the road and come to BOARD NO. 9. Below, there is a lovely grassy area beside the river, ideal for picnicking (Picnic 17). The way onward from Board No. 9 is not obvious. You must cross the field, heading slightly uphill, to reach the shrubby trees where you will pick up the waymarks again.

Between Boards No. 9 and 10 you will see a DEPTH GAUGE fixed to a tree. Amazingly, the 9m-level is just above head height! Drop down to another field. BOARD NO. 10 is up to your left, so follow the field edge to reach it. From here a faint path crosses the field and re-enters the wood. Continue on, passing BOARD NO. 11 to reach BOARD NO. 12. From here, walk down onto the river bank to see Veliki Naravni Most. The collapsed caves have left this natural bridge (which you drove over earlier, if you came via Postojna) standing proud; the precision-cut of the rock by the river Rak is incredible and looks almost man-made. Return to Board No. 12 and climb the steps to reach the road once more. Turn right here and, after a sharp right-hand bend, look for BOARD NO. 13 on your left. Do not skip by, but take a closer look!

Below you is a **Tkalca Jama** and inside it, the river Rak. (Optional: If you take care and are sure-footed, you can descend into this cavern to the river below and see the main entrance to the cave. The inside can be very slippery and dangerous if the river is high; when in flood it can reach the roadside entrance! The Rak rushes by and disappears noisily into a dark underground channel once more.)

The main walk continues along the road to cross **Veliki Naravni Most**. There are viewpoints on both sides and fences to keep you from the edge. At the far side of this natural bridge a path climbs a few metres to the church of **Sv. Kancijan (55min)**. It is almost completely in ruins but, in one small part, we were moved to find a crucifix and a lighted candle on an old stone altar.

Return to the road and turn left. After 80m look for a (red/white) waymarked path down to the right. This soon becomes a wide path and leads to a gravel road in two minutes. Turn right and follow this road for 2km, passing BOARD NO. 2. At the next junction, turn left to return almost immediately to the **Rakov Škocjan** CAR PARK (**1h26min**).

Distance/time: 12km/7.5mi; 2h45min
Grade: easy; on country roads
Equipment: see page 38; walking shoes

How to get there: 🚌 or 🚃 to Rogaška Slatina
Nearest accommodation: Rogaška Slatina

Quiet country roads take you on an easy ramble through an area of mixed farming and vineyards. Our walk visits the village and church of Sv. Florjan, the patron saint of firemen. As you travel about Slovenia you can see him pictured hard at work on many fire stations. Take a picnic to enjoy by the church, which will tell you in no uncertain terms when it's lunchtime!

Set out from the TOURIST INFOR-MATION CENTRE on the corner of CELJSKA CESTA and ZDRAVILIŠKI TRG in **Rogaška Slatina**. Walk up through the ornamental gardens past the imposing Zdraviliški Dom. The round building at the end of the square is the Drinking Hall. Walk to the right of the high-rise therapy building, which is out of keeping with the grandeur of the surrounding architecture, and go under a walkway. Keep straight ahead from here and cross a road. Take the right-hand, lower, of the two roads ahead, passing the car park and following the sign to DONAČKA GORA. Ignore a fork off to the left and walk by the Sports Centre on your right, to escape the hustle and bustle of the town. The road climbs a little, to a junction (**15min**). Go straight on, passing an old WATER PUMP and a TARGET MARK on a garden fence (both on your right).

Still on the road, walk by houses and through fields to reach, after another nine minutes, a junction beside a CRUCIFIX. Here turn right over a bridge across a wide ditch, to continue along the road. You soon pass an old barn and reach another junction (**30min**). Turn left and walk through **Tuncovec**, a scattered collection of houses and old farm buildings.

As you leave this hamlet, keep straight on until you come to Rogaška Slatina's BYPASS (**42min**). Cross the bypass, and head along the road signposted to SV. FLORJAN. The wooded but shapely peak of Donačka Gora can be seen ahead. Follow this road as it winds its way through the fields and climbs up a small hill with a farm at the top. Carry on past a building with a painting of Sv. Florjan and cross a small bridge decorated with flowers. About 20 minutes from the bypass, turn left at a junction, to reach another junction two minutes later. The main road bears round to the right, but you must keep straight on beside a beech wood. Soon you will see the church of Sv. Florjan in the distance. At a T-junction opposite HOUSE NO. 83 (**1h22min**), turn left into **Sv. Florjan**. Below the church go right, up the short but steep hill, and then turn left to reach the CHURCH (**1h27min**). There is a good grassy area nearby to enjoy a break.

Continue down from the church entrance to meet the main village road again. You soon pass a *gasilski dom* (fire station) with its painting of Sv. Florjan, before the road climbs through a wood. From the top of the hill you now begin a gentle descent through the

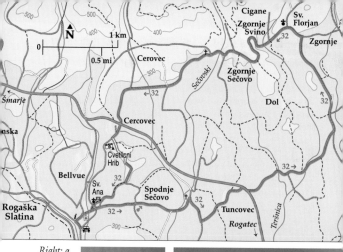

Right: a wind rattle (klopotci) for scaring birds; far right: stacks of maize line the road at Sv. Florjan.

long village of **Zgornje Sečovo**. In the village ignore a turn off to the right followed by another to the left. Beyond the houses ignore yet another turn to the right (there is a shrine about 100m along this road) and keep on the main road, going under a POWER LINE (**1h50min**). Continue straight ahead through a crossroads (**1h58min**). A few minutes further on, just after a turn to the right, the road bends to the left by a garden centre and descends easily to the BYPASS (**2h13min**), by a bar.

Cross on the zebra crossing and go up the road opposite (signposted to ROGAŠKA SLATINA), bearing left up a narrow road and then keeping right after one minute. The road soon becomes a gravel track, and there is a fine view back along your route. Walk up and around to the far side of a little hill, **Cvetlicni Hrib**. At the track's highest point (**2h22min**), a

narrow path climbs a few feet to a shady VIEWPOINT overlooking vineyards and the outskirts of Rogaška Slatina. Continue down the track, which soon becomes an asphalt road again, between the houses (one has a painting on it of Donačka Gora). On a sharp left-hand bend, turn right down a track. (After a few metres look back, to see the name 'Ivanov Hrib' on a sign on a tree.) Continue down the track, which passes a few houses and then becomes asphalt. About 75m after a sharp left-hand bend, take a track off right into the trees; it passes to the left of a sheltered picnic table. Drop down a steep bank, then follow 'NO. 3' signs to the chapel of **Sv. Ana** (**2h38min**). Descend the steps to cross a road and make your way to the Drinking Hall, which is just opposite. Retrace your steps along ZDRAVILIŠKI TRG to the TOURIST INFORMATION CENTRE (**2h45min**).

Distance/time: 7km/4.4mi; 1h48min
Grade: easy, on country roads
Equipment: see page 38; walking shoes
How to get there: 🚗 Drive 4km

south from Podčetrtek and turn right in Golobinjek. Follow the valley's main road for another 4km to park near Gostišče Virštanj.
Nearest accommodation: Podčetrtek , Rogaška Slatina

Here you are in the heart of wine country, walking through the vineyards, perfect for an autumn day when the grapes are being harvested. What can be better than sampling the local vintage at a delightful wine house near the end of this ramble — you only have a further 2km to saunter back to your car!

To start the walk, head along the road from the *GOSTIŠČE VIRŠTANJ* towards Podčetrtek. After nine minutes, opposite a *SHRINE* dated 1994, turn left up a narrow asphalt road. Ignore a farm road on the left, and then drop slightly beside the vines before climbing up past farms and orchards. Just after HOUSE NO. 59 you reach a junction

Below: the church of Sv. Filip and Jakob at Sela; opposite: grapes ready for harvest in October (top) and the view from Sv. Filip and Jakob to the Golobinjski Valley

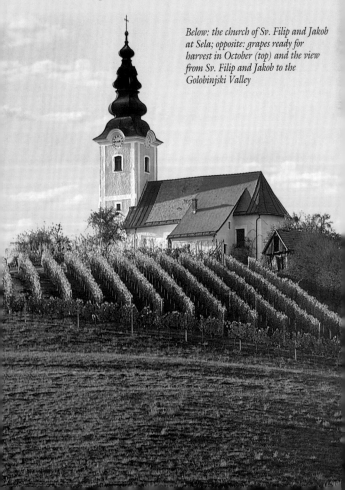

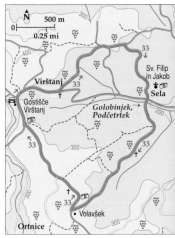

(**24min**). Ignore the uphill road on your left and carry straight on beside farm buildings. In 200m, where the road forks, take the left-hand branch, slightly uphill. After a short climb the road descends past a farm to another junction, where you turn right downhill, under POWER LINES. (Look out for the wind rattle or *klopotci*, a bird-scarer similar to the one shown on page 115).

You now wind downhill through vines and, after going under a large weeping willow, walk between fields. Eventually you come into **Sela** (**42min**) where, at the end of a short track you will find the little church of **Sv. Filip and Jakob**. Sitting atop a small hill, the church seems to be almost part of the neighbouring farm. On the south-facing slopes, vines fan out down the hill — a lovely foreground for your views of the Golobinjski Valley.

Return to the road and descend left to reach the MAIN VALLEY ROAD (**48min**). Go straight across and follow the narrow road that climbs the hillside opposite. Pass a large, and not particularly attractive farm building on the left and some white houses on the right. Keep straight on, walking under the POWER LINES again. Beyond a decorated CRUCIFIX you climb up through more vineyards to a large, old GRAPE PRESS. At the next junction is **Volavšek** (**1h22min**), a wine house with fine paintings on its walls. The friendly host will be more than delighted for you to sample his wine. We recommend the white and the home-baked *potica* (a traditional cake with a variety of fillings).

Turn right at the junction and soon pass a beautiful SHRINE. There are tranquil views over the valley — what an idyllic place to live! After a small wood you gently descend to another junction, where you turn right. Enjoy the fine views back down to Sela as you return to the GOSTIŠČE VIRŠTANJ (**1h48min**).

34 ROGLA • SEDLO KOMISIJA • MULEJEV VRH • LOVRENŠKA JEZERA • SEDLO KOMISIJA • ROGLA

See also photograph page 13
Distance/time: 9km/5.6mi; 2h12min
Grade: easy; mainly on good forest paths
Equipment: see page 38; walking boots
How to get there: 🚐 from Zreče or 🚗: leave the A1

Ljubljana/Maribor motorway at the exit for Zreče and Rogla. Drive through Slovenske Konjice and then turn right up to Zreče. Now follow signs for Rogla, 14km/8.75mi up a winding road.
Nearest accommodation: Zreče, Celje

This walk on the Pohorje Massif is based around the popular skiing and fitness centre of Rogla. At a height of 1500m/4920ft you will have your fill of clear mountain air. Be careful not to disturb the water in the small pools of the Lovrenška Jezera, as you may upset the goblin, Jezernik. He brings on bad weather when angry!

Start from the HOTEL PLANJA in **Rogla**: cross the main road and walk between some wooden huts and past a large signpost to reach the TOP OF THE CHAIRLIFT. From here take a grassy track across open pasture; white signposts mark the way. There are several tracks heading up the far slope, but you must aim for the one on the left. After climbing gently for eight minutes you reach a small WAR MEMORIAL. In another four minutes, near the top of **Ostruščica**, a small rounded hill, bear left (signposted 'JEZERO'). The path now descends gradually, with open views across the massif to the west and northwest (Picnic 20, photograph page 13). You come to **Sedlo Komisija** (**22min**), a broad, flat, marshy area that you must cross. (If it is too wet, bear right before the bog to a track, turn left and, in less than one minute, bear left again at another fork to climb up to the main route.)

From the far side of the bog a path climbs easily through the forest, joining the alternative path coming in from the right. After nine minutes you reach another open area, again with fine views. The easy path keeps to the west of **Mulejev Vrh** before descending gently through trees (where you will see many large anthills). Eventually you come to a junction (**56min**); turn right uphill following clear signposting to the lakes. In a further five minutes you reach the OBSERVATION TOWER shown left. Climb to the top for the best view of the **Lovrenška Jezera**, this strange marshy area. There are information boards (unfortunately all in Slovenian) detailing the flora and fauna. The board of 'Do's and Don'ts', however, is plain enough! Follow the BOARDWALK to the centre of the lakes area, where you will see some deep, dark pools. But remember Jezernik and tread carefully! Then retrace your steps back to the OBSERVATION TOWER (**1h11min**).

To return, cross the rather wet area by the tower and turn left into the trees along a path, indicated by NO. 1 TARGET MARKS. Look out for black squirrels as you follow the well-defined path to a track junction (**1h44min**). Confusingly, both forks here are waymarked with No. 1 Target marks. But keep to the right-hand fork, signposted for the HOTEL PLANJA.

In four minutes you come to a bench where a track joins from the right. Keep straight on (**Sedlo Komisija** is just a little higher to your right) passing a yellow 'PP2' on a tree and walking steadily uphill. You reach your outward route at the top of the ridge by a bench. Turn left to pass the small MEMORIAL and return to HOTEL PLANJA in **Rogla** (**2h12min**).

Left: the boardwalk from the observation tower to the Lovrenška Jezera

35 ŠPORT HOTEL AREH • VELIKI ŠUMIK • ŠPORT HOTEL AREH

Distance/time: 15km/9.4mi; 3h48min

Grade: moderate-strenuous. The walk is mostly on easy unsurfaced roads, forest tracks and paths, but the descent to the waterfalls crosses steep ground and can be wet and slippery. On this scramble you will need to use your hands and have a head for heights.

Equipment: see page 38; walking boots

How to get there: 🚗 Just north of the end of the A1 motorway to Maribor follow signs for Hoče and Areh. A long twisting ascent leads in 18km/11.25mi to Areh.

Short walk: Veliki Šumik. 1.5km/0.9mi; 50min. Grade and equipment as main walk. Access: Follow the directions above and drive to the end of the car park. Take the unsurfaced road and bear right after 750m to continue on, ignoring three turns to the right. At a left turn after 4.5km, keep right and then go right again, to park at a picnicking area beside the river. Follow the main walk from the 1h22min-point to Veliki Šumik and back.

Nearest accommodation: Maribor, Ptuj, Celje

The heavily-wooded Pohorje Massif, the 'lungs of Maribor', is a popular spot for Slovenians all year round. In the heart of this area lies one of Eastern Slovenia's beauty spots, the Šumik Waterfalls, hidden deep in virgin forest.

Begin at the far end of the CAR PARK by the ŠPORT HOTEL AREH. Head west through the trees along the road and reach a CLEARING (**9min**). Turn left on a wide path, clearly waymarked with a TARGET MARK and a NO. 1. We follow these markings almost all the way to the falls.

The path traverses the hillside and then descends gently, eventually reaching a road (**34min**). Cross this to continue around the left of a grassy field. The way is easily followed, but you must keep a sharp look out for the target marks at all times. After 22 minutes pass a small MEMORIAL on the left, just before you reach a track on a bend near Tinčeva Bajta. Take a path a few metres to the right of the memorial; it leads to a road in four minutes (**59min**).

Go straight across the road and walk along the track opposite, to reach a small, circular GRASSY CLEARING. On the far side the path climbs through a deep rut and then continues gently uphill to a

fine beech wood with amazingly tall, straight trees. The path, rough in places, now descends quite steeply to a road. Cross this, to quickly come to another road. Turn left to reach a BRIDGE over a small river, where there is a PICNIC AREA (**1h22min**). *(The Short walk starts here.)*

Leaving the No. 1 target marks behind, cross the bridge and turn right down into the trees. With a river on either side, follow the signs for VELIKI and MALI SLAP (great and little waterfalls), to cross the river on your right via a FOOTBRIDGE. Continue above the riverbank. This is a rather wet area, and the wooden boardwalks are not in good repair.

The nature of the walk changes dramatically from here, and *care is needed*. On the steep hillside you must negotiate tree roots and rocky areas where you will find metal foot- and hand-holds in places. You need to be sure-footed, and this is just a taste of things to come! The most difficult

120

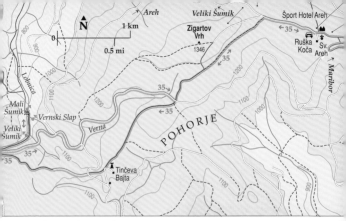

part of the walk is the descent to the 'Great Falls', but there are cables to hold and guide you down the steep slope to the BASE OF **Veliki Šumik** (**1h46min**). The river **Lobnica** cascades down stepped rocks and the scene is made more dramatic by the atmospheric *pragozd* (primeval forest). Here the trees have never been harvested, giving the impression that you are in an ancient lost world.

(*Optional:* one *can* descend further downstream to reach the lower falls in about 20 minutes, but we found the path in a very poor state on our last visit — it had even slipped into the river at one point. The path crosses a bridge, beyond which you have to scramble along and down to the base of Mali Šumik. These falls are quite different, and it is difficult to get good views of the river as it flows down a narrow chute.)

The main and short walks return from Veliki Šumik. Retrace your steps to the road and PICNIC AREA (**2h12min**; *the Short walk ends here*) and turn left to reach the little path that you descended earlier. While you can return to Areh the way you came, the main walk takes a different route. Carry on up the road, to quickly reach a junction. Turn left here (signposted for AREH) and walk along the road that runs above the river seen far below. After 15

Veliki Šumik — the 'Great Falls'

minutes you come to a junction. Turn right towards 'SLOVENSKA BISTRICA' (do *not* go left for Areh), and follow the road for eight minutes, to another junction. Turn left now (signposted to AREH) and follow this road uphill for 2.5km to meet your outward route at the 34min-point (**3h12min**). Turn left and return to the ŠPORT HOTEL AREH (**3h48min**).

See also photos pages 2, 34-35
Distance/time: 12.5km/7.8mi; 4h10min
Grade: moderate-strenuous; on good tracks and paths, starting with an ascent of 210m/680ft but ending with a descent of 1100m/3575ft
Equipment: see page 38; walking boots, walking sticks. Refreshments are available, in season, from the many mountain huts en route.
How to get there: 🚌 Drive north from Kamnik, following signs for the Velika Planina cable car, as far as the junction in Stahovica. Park here and catch the Kamniška Bistrica 🚌, which stops at the cable car station, or walk the 5km/3mi along the road. The bus runs three times a day, the buses at 7.00 and 11.30 (not weekends) being the most suitable. Or 🚌 From Ljubljana to Kamnik, then catch the bus to Kamniška Bistrica (as above). Obtain up-to-date bus and cable car schedules at the tourist information centre in Kamnik.
Nearest accommodation: Kamnik
Shorter walk: Velika Planina — Gojška Planina — Mala Planina — Velika Planina. 10km/6.3km; 2h51min. Quite easy; ascents/descents of about 320m/1050ft overall. Equipment as main walk. Access: 🚌 From Kamnik follow directions given above and then turn left at the junction in

Stahovica. Park at the cable car station, which is 5km along this road. 🚌 As above to the cable car station. Follow the main walk to the junction at the 1h42min-point. Turn right, and then left at the next junction, to climb back up to Dom na Velika Planina. From here retrace your steps to the upper cable car station.
Alternative walk: Stahovica — Sv. Primož and Sv. Peter — Stahovica. 6km/3.8m; 2h15min. Quite easy; on good paths and tracks with a total ascent and descent of 400m/1300ft. Equipment as main walk. Access by 🚌 or 🚌 to Stahovica as main walk. From the junction walk up the road towards Črna, to the shrine shown above. A path starts here. Climb this to a gravel road, cross over, and continue on the path until it meets the road again. Keep up the road past some farms, then take a short-cut path to the right. Meeting the road again, turn right for 40m and, from the hairpin bend, follow a track to Sv. Primož and Sv. Peter, perched on the end of a ridge with a pleasant sunny outlook. The bar, where you can ask for the keys to see the wonderful frescoes in Sv. Primož, is full of artefacts of yesteryear and you are assured of a friendly welcome. Return the same way.

Photo: walkers' shrine at Stahovica

A visit to Velika Planina, a snow sports area and one of the largest summer pastures for the traditional dairy farmer, is a unique experience. Although not the original buildings, the design of the houses dates back many generations. They are small and low with rounded walls and conical roofs, silver grey in colour. Cows, with their tinkling bells, graze the well-cropped pastures where cowslips and other wild flowers flourish. The panoramic views from this high plateau are breathtaking. 'The Great Highlands' are a favourite outing for Slovenians and you will soon understand why — we almost started yodelling at the sheer magnificence of it all!

Starting from the UPPER CABLE CAR STATION, take the track past the GOSTIŠČE ŠIMNOVEC TRENO-ČIŠČA. The first part of the walk follows the chairlift so, after eight minutes, keep straight on where the motorable track goes off left. Climb the slope ahead, first to the right of the chairlift and then to the left. You come to the motorable track again and go over a cattle grid. Bear slightly left here, up to the huts and another bar at **Zeleni Rob** (**30min**), where you will find a distinctive signpost, the branched trunk of an old tree. Take the wide track ahead that contours the hillside. Scattered in the trees to your left are some of the houses and buildings unique to this area. After five minutes, at another signposted junction, bear left; in a further four minutes you reach a SKI LIFT.*

Leave the main track here and, after walking around a large crater, you will meet the first of the distinctive houses of **Velika Planina**. This small hamlet is set in a hollow, with a tiny church on a little hillock behind it. Walk down the grassy track through the scattered dwellings to **Kapela Marije Snežne** (Our Lady of the Snows), ideally situated to enjoy views over Velika Planina to the Kamniško-Savinjske Alps (**54min**).

With your back to the church bear

left down the grassy slope, to reach a track by one of the most attractive houses, which has a pond behind it. There is another distinctive signpost here (photographs on pages 2, 34-35). Turn left, and after seven minutes bear left at a fork. Beyond a TURNSTILE GATE, the path passes just by the front door of the DOM NA VELIKA PLANINA (**1h06min**). Continue on a gravel track and in one minute come to a junction. Turn left here. Keep on this track, passing JARŠKI DOM, and zigzag down to another junction (**1h14min**). Turn left again and follow the track through a small area of trees, to emerge at the top of **Gojška Planina**. Go through a TURNSTILE GATE to reach a junction (**1h24min**), where you turn sharp right and walk down through an idyllic scene of herdsmen's houses and grazing cattle. Look out for some artistic features — a roof ridge piece looks like a cow's head and you may see an unusual table with three legs. Traditional cheeses are still made here throughout the summer, and the farmers are very friendly. At the bottom of the hill, opposite a POOL and another impressive signpost, turn right uphill. Go through a gate and continue, following TARGET MARKS where the track becomes less clear, up to another track (**1h42min**). Cross

*Mist can descend quickly, and if this happens we suggest that you take a different route to Velika Planina: follow the main track beside this ski lift to the left. The track goes by some buildings on the right and after seven minutes

passes under another ski tow. Two minutes later, at a junction, turn right into **Velika Planina**. Walk between the first two houses on your left and then to the right of the next two buildings. The church is 150m further on.

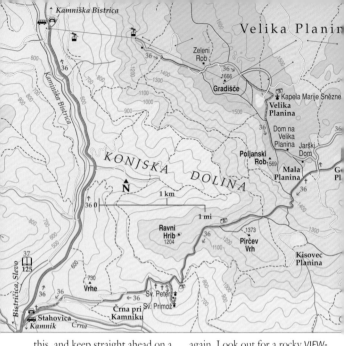

this, and keep straight ahead on a faint grassy path behind the first houses of **Mala Planina**. Walk between the buildings into a wide grassy area where there is a small CRUCIFIX. Your descent starts by the last visible telegraph pole ahead, beside a signpost to KISOVEC (**1h49min**).

Follow the path downhill, soon joining another coming in from the right, and continue down the well-used and sometimes badly-eroded path. It doubles back sharply; a minute later, ignore a path dropping steeply to the left. Here you will meet the first signs for STAHOVICA. Continue straight on to a junction on a COL, in some lovely old beech trees (**2h10min**). Take the right fork (the left fork goes over the summit of Pirčev Vrh and rejoins us later), and traverse under the wooded hilltop. The path is narrow and a bit vertiginous in places, but it is not difficult and affords fine views over the steep wooded slopes (colourful in autumn) below Velika Planina. The path regains the ridge for a few metres before descending

124

again. Look out for a rocky VIEW-POINT with good vistas over Kamnik and beyond. Meeting another wide path (**3h**), turn left to the churches of **Sv. Primož** and **Sv. Peter** (**3h10min**), described in the Alternative walk on page 122).

Return to the junction and continue downhill, soon passing SHRINES, the first one leaning, the second beautifully painted. Eleven minutes from the junction, you meet a gravel road. Turn left and then almost immediately left again, back on to a wide path, which ends at the gravel road in only four minutes. Follow the road downhill past some attractive farms with flower-filled window boxes. At a sharp left-hand bend, take a short-cut right, down through the trees (at one point in what looks like a wide ditch). When you meet the road again, go straight over and follow the path, above the rear of some houses, to join the road by the SHRINE shown on page 122. Turn right; the junction in **Stahovica** is just a minute away (**4h10min**).

37 SLEVO • KAMNIŠKI VRH • PLANJAVA •
PLANINA OSREDEK • RAVNE SENOŽETI • SLEVO

Distance/time: 7.5km/4.7mi; 3h03min

Grade: strenuous; on good paths, but with a steep ascent of 700m/2300ft. An alternative (steep and slippery) descent is possible, which shortens the walk by 2km and 30min. See footnote page 126.

Equipment: see page 38; walking boots, walking sticks

How to get there: 🚗 Drive north from Kamnik for 5km/3mi, following signs for Velika Planina. At the entrance to Stahovica, turn left beside the 'Bistro'. Cross a bridge, and then another with a shrine nearby. Turn left here and follow the stream uphill to Bistričica. Do not enter the village, but cross the bridge. after 2.2km/1.4mi and two more stream crossings, park near a bridge with metal railings, at the start of a motorable track to Slevo. 🚌 From Kamnik to Stahovica. Then walk the 2.8km/1.7mi to the starting point, following the instructions above.

Nearest accommodation: Kamnik

Short walk: Slevo — hunters' cabin — Ravne Senoženi — Slevo. 4.3km/2.7mi; 1h29min. Easy; equipment and access as main walk. Follow the main walk to the T-junction at the 48min-point. Turn left (but first walk another five minutes to the right, to enjoy the view from the ridge), and traverse the hillside, to enter the trees that hide a wide but easily-crossed gully. At the far side, turn left on a path to reach a hut, and then descend to the right at a fork, to rejoin the main walk beside a red signpost. Now follow the main walk from the 2h32min-point to the end.

A steep ascent through woodland takes you to an unusual grass-covered mountain with a bristle of trees along its ridge — we liken it to a dragon. When you have toiled up to his head, you must tackle his tail — a bumpy ridge with tussocky knolls. After your hard climb, the descent is a treat.

Start by crossing the BRIDGE and walking up the gravel road to **Slevo**, a small collection of houses and a farm. Your objective is in full view and looks a little daunting from here. Follow the road past an unusual WAR MEMORIAL to a rough PARKING AREA. Some 20m beyond it, the track forks (**15min**). The left fork, signposted for Kamniški Vrh, is our return route on the descent, but also the way to turn for Picnic 22.

The main walk bears *right* here, along a clear track that heads up into the trees (*no* waymarks). Follow the track steadily uphill, to two HUNTERS' CABINS (**40min**). Turn left, passing to the right of a picnic table, to take a narrow grassy path that heads onto the open hillside. In eight minutes, beyond a SMALL METAL CROSS, turn right at a T-junction (**48min**).

On the ridge of Kamniški Vrh

(*The Short walk turns left here.*) The path traverses and climbs gently along to the ridge, where there is a good VIEWPOINT (**53min**). From here the slopes seem ever steeper, and you can see the path that you must climb to the summit ridge. The hard work ends beside a small WOODEN BIVOUAC and a few welcome benches. The top is only two minutes further on in the trees, so rest here and enjoy the views over Kamnik and beyond. To the west are the higher hills of Kržišče and Krvavec while behind, glimpsed through the trees, are the Kamniško-Savinjske Alps. To the east is Velika Planina.

Carry on to the SUMMIT OF **Kamniški Vrh** (**1h23min**) and sign the visitors' book. Ahead is a neighbouring but lower peak, with a bristle of beech trees. To reach it you must first descend to a COL (**1h29min**).* Then climb again up the grassy slopes to reach the TOP OF **Planjava** (**1h41min**).

From the rounded summit descend the ridge on a path that winds between the trees at the edge of the wood. Look out for the enormous anthills around here and check very carefully if you sit down to rest! The path continues along the ridge crest over a few bumps to reach a signpost on a wooded COL (**1h57min**).

Turn left towards PLANINA OSREDEK and descend through more beech trees. Just by a rickety old fence, and before the *planina*, an ARROW AND TARGET MARK indicate a left turn. Take this, passing two old wooden HUTS, and then turn left again when you join a path coming in from the *planina* on your right (there is a 'KAMNIŠKI VRH' TARGET MARK on a very old beech tree in front of you). Very soon you pass a CRUCIFIX with a viewpoint behind it (**2h09min**).

A minute later you reach a fork. The right branch, the path indicated on Slovenian maps, has suffered a landslide, so fork *left*, towards SLEVO. This narrow path traverses the steep hillside and is somewhat vertiginous. After 13 minutes you go through a TURN-STILE GATE into an area of shrubby trees. After another TURNSTILE you enter thicker woodland, but you soon reach a grassy area, called **Ravne Senožeti**.

Keep left to meet a wide path (which climbs to the col between the two summits) at a RED SIGN-POST (**2h32min**; *the Short walk and the alternative descent rejoin the main walk here*). Turn right, down-hill, and enjoy the wild flowers of the hay meadows. Across the valley on the opposite hillside is Zakal with its little church of Sv. Florjan. The path keeps to the right of the field and becomes a gravel track before descending a bit more steeply to the junction at the 15min-point on the outward route (**2h51min**). Continue on the main track round to the right to reach **Slevo** and return to your car (**3h03min**).

---

*To shorten the walk by 2km (30min), turn left from this col on a path that quickly descends to the top of a gully. Descend the *very steep, eroded and slippery path* beside the gully. After 25 minutes ignore a path going left into the trees and, four minutes later, reach a hut at the top of a large grassy area. At the fork in front of the hut descend to the right, to rejoin the main walk at a red signpost. Follow the main walk from the 2h32min-point to the end.

38 ROBANOV KOT • ROBANOVA PLANINA • ROBANOV KOT

See also photograph page 34
Distance/time: 9km/5.6mi;
1h50min
Grade: easy, on well-surfaced
tracks
Equipment: see page 38; walking
shoes. In season refreshments are
available from a hut in Robanova
Planina.
How to get there: 🚗 Turn left in
Robanov Kot, just before the road
bridge across the Savinja River,
and follow this narrow road for
750m to a large parking area in
the trees. 🚌 From Celje. Alight
opposite the Gostišče Rogovlic in
Robanov Kot. Cross the footbridge over the river and turn left
uphill. At the narrow asphalt road
turn right and, in six minutes,
come to the parking area.
Nearest accommodation:
Logarska Dolina, Celje
**Alternative walk: Robanov Kot
— Partizanska Bolnica —
Robanov Kot.** 4km/2.5mi;
1h30min. Moderate, with a very
steep climb of 200m/650ft. Equipment: walking boots, walking
sticks. Access as above. Follow the
main walk to the 17min-point.

Take the left fork, signposted for
the partisans' hospital, Partizanska
Bolnica, and head across the dry
riverbed. Aim for a large rock,
which is upstream and straight
ahead. On it are some faded paint
marks and letters, indicating that
you are on the correct route. Keep
straight on to the far bank, where
you will see target marks on the
trees. A red arrow indicates the
start of the path. The narrow, well
waymarked path zigzags steeply
uphill into a ever-more-constricted
gully. Just when you start to
wonder if you will ever be able to
climb further, the path escapes to
the left, traversing across a steep,
rocky slope, where you will need
to take care, before climbing
again. Eventually you reach a little
promontory where there is a
bird's-eye view down into the
lower part of Robanov Kot. Climb
for a few more metres and then
traverse the slopes, to reach the
well-hidden remains of the WWII
hospital shown overleaf, which
shelters below a rocky outcrop.
Return the same way.

Robanov Kot is no less beautiful than Logarska Dolina, the adjacent and much-publicised valley, but is much more peaceful and less frequented. The grazings of Robanova Planina sit near the base of sheer cliffs and high mountains and are a wonderful place to while away a sunny afternoon. If you are looking for more of a physical challenge, the main walk and the Alternative walk, which visits the remains of a partisans' hospital, can easily be combined — allow just under an hour extra.

Start out at the PARKING AREA in
Robanov Kot. Walk up the road,
passing the farm shown overleaf,
Govc. Already the mountains at
the head of the valley dominate the
view, Ojstrica being the highest.
The asphalt road ends at the
attractive farm of **Roban**, where
you follow the TARGET MARKS

between the buildings, first
turning right and then left onto a
track. Just above the farm you can
see a BEEHIVE HUT (**9min**).
Continue along the track and, after
four minutes, ignore a track that
goes off left towards the river.
Soon after you reach a junction.
Go straight ahead here, past the

Above: Govc farm in Robanov Kot, backed by the high mountains at the head of the valley. Below left: Partizanska Bolnica, the partisans' hospital, hidden in the trees. There is one reconstructed hut, with two framed drawings inside, and some bunk beds. You will also see other, ruined huts and a plaque. The hospital was only used for a short time from September 1944 to January 1945.

green and white BARRIER AND NOTICE BOARD. In a further two minutes you reach another junction (**17min**) beside the river bed, which is dry for most of the year. This is the pleasant setting for Picnic 23a. *(The Alternative walk forks left here.)*

Keep right, following the track, which soon leaves the river bed by climbing a short, steep incline. You walk beside a field, where you may see ponies used for hauling timber from the adjoining woods, and reach an old BARN (**30min**), dating from 1912. Just beyond is

128

some open pasture (Picnic 23b). The track continues on into the trees and heads gently uphill. You may see black squirrels here. After 18 minutes go through a wooden gate and in another four minutes leave the trees to enter **Robanova Planina** — a most dramatic scene! Walk on to arrive at HOUSE NO. 36 (**55min**) where, in the summer, you can buy refreshments. This is another ideal picnic spot, surrounded by high mountains that tower over you on three sides. It is possible to pick out the alpine route that breaches the cliffs at the lowest part of the skyline on the left.

To return, retrace your steps to **Robanov Kot** (**1h50min**), enjoying the views down the valley to the high mountain of Velika Raduha.

Distance/time: 15km/9.4mi; 3h51min

Grade: easy, mainly on good paths

Equipment: see page 38; walking shoes. There are several inns along the route and a snack bar at the Slap Rinka car park.

How to get there: 🚗 Park in the car park, 300m before the entrance to the Logarska Dolina Park, or in the lay-by opposite the church. 🚌 From Celje. Get off at the entrance to Logarska Dolina Park.

Nearest accommodation: Logarska Dolina, Celje

Short walk: It is possible to get a bus either up or down the valley, halving the walking distance. This service is, however, limited.

Logarska Dolina, one of the most beautiful glacial valleys in Europe, has a wonderful ambience. Despite its popularity, you can still escape the crowds by walking only a short way from the car parks. Relax in the quiet serenity of the protected woodlands, learn about ancient crafts and enjoy the ever-changing light on the mountain peaks.

Begin the walk at the PARK KIOSK: walk down the road, through open fields. After nearly 1km the road crosses a stream and, beside the bridge on the left, there is a small parking area. Your onward path starts on the opposite side of the road and is clearly signposted 'POT PO LOGARSKI' (**17min**). A SYMBOL WITH THE FIGURE OF A WALKER now leads you most of the way to the head of the valley.

Follow the path between two streams, and then bear right into the trees to cross a little footbridge near **Izvir Črne**, the source of the river Črna. Here you will see the first of the INFORMATION BOARDS, in English, which you will find at every point of interest. Continue up the valley to reach the edge of a field (**27min**; Picnic 24), from where there are good views of the mountains and a diagram to help with orientation. A little further on you reach a FORESTERS' HUT with a wooden log shoot behind it, and some picnic tables.

In another nine minutes you come to BOARD NO. 5 (about birds), where you *leave* the main signposted route. Turn left, and then immediately right, to follow the river (dry for most of the year),

until you reach a footbridge. Cross this and then go straight across the road that is just ahead. A track takes you up to the HOTEL PLESNIK (**42min**), at the back of which is **Slap Palenk**. Enjoy the mountain views as you walk from the hotel along the asphalt road between open, grassy fields. After six minutes you reach DOMACIJA PLESNIK, where you bear right on a gravel track. Follow this to meet the MAIN VALLEY ROAD by PENSION NA RAZPOTJU (**54min**).

Turn left up the road. After approximately 100m your signposted onward path crosses the road. Turn left again and follow this path for six minutes, to BOARD NO. 7. Here, look out for the tallest juniper tree in Slovenia; you may not be impressed by its height, but remember that these trees are usually no more than low bushes. Soon you meet the road again (**1h07min**). Go behind the INN opposite and then on to a CHARCOAL BURNERS' HUT. There are more picnic tables here, albeit somewhat sooty! Next you come to the riverbed: follow this, keeping to the right. After seven minutes you cross a side stream and then the river bed by BOARD

129

Autumn colours in Logarska Dolina

NO. 11 and reach the road. Go directly opposite on a track up to PLANŠARIA LOGARSKI KOT, where there is another parking area (**1h27min**). Turn right just before the inn, over a STILE and into the woods. You quickly come to a field, which is sometimes used as a football pitch. Cross it by bearing right, to find another STILE which takes you into the trees again. Soon the path divides (both forks are marked with the 'WALKER' SYMBOL). Turn right and follow the path to the road (**1h39min**). Walk uphill to the lay-by opposite and take the rough track from here back up to the road, cutting out a bend. Go straight across and, from the track, you will have a spectacular view of the upper part of Logarska Dolina on the far side of the wide gravely river bed. Slap Rinka is just visible, and a BOARD identifies the peaks. Continue along this track through beech woods, forking right after five minutes, to cross the river bed on a footbridge and reach the TOP CAR PARK (**1h53min**).

Now follow the notes at the beginning of Walk 40 (opposite) to continue on to **Slap Rinka** (**2h03min**).

If you are walking back down the valley, retrace your steps to the road crossing near the PENSION NA RAZPOTJU. From here, you can simply reverse your outward journey back to the PARK KIOSK (**3h51min**). Alternatively, cross the road and follow the signposted route back (this is slightly quicker and includes BOARD NO. 6, but is much less scenic), to rejoin the main walk at BOARD NO. 5.

See map opposite
Distance/time: 3.3km/2mi;
2h09min
Grade: moderate; on good
mountain paths, with an initial
steep ascent of 400m/1300ft
Equipment: see page 38; walking
boots, walking sticks Refreshments are available from Okrešlju
Dom in season.
How to get there: 🚗 Park in the
car park at the head of Logarska
Dolina. 🚌 from Celje; there is a
limited service to the start of this
walk.
Nearest accommodation:
Logarska Dolina, Celje

*The Savinjško Sedlo path behind the
Okrešlju Dom leads through this lovely
clearing with wonderful views over the
trees to the surrounding peaks of the
Kamniško-Savinjske Alps.*

You may already have visited Slap Rinka (Walk 39), but to
continue above it is to enter a different world. You climb
up from the main valley to a small amphitheatre of jagged
peaks rising steeply on three sides — peaks so white that they
are almost blue! The descent through beech woods is wonderful, especially in autumn, when the colours are stunning.

Begin at the CAR PARK: take the
path signposted 'SLAP RINKA',
opposite a little bar. A steady but
easy climb brings you to a FOOT-
BRIDGE over a stream, at the foot
of the waterfall. From this vantage
point **Slap Rinka** (**10min**) seems
to flow directly from the blue sky.
To the right and up some steps is a
small bar with a balcony overlooking the falls.
Cross the bridge and walk up the
steep, but stepped, path through
the trees. The first stage of the
climb ends at the top of the waterfall, where you cross a FOOTBRIDGE
and continue up a flight of
wooden steps (with a handrail).
The path winds up through
boulders, passing a turn to the
right (your return path), and a
minute later you arrive at **Izvir
Savinje** (**39min**), the source of
the river **Savinja**. The water issues
from beneath some large rocks to
begin its long journey to the
Black Sea via the Danube.
The way is easier now and con-

tinues through beech trees to reach
the OKREŠLJU DOM (**54min**). Treat
yourself to a refreshing drink while
sitting on the balcony overlooking
the valley below.
Then take the path from the back
of the *dom*, signposted to
SAVINJSKO SEDLO. It leads through
the grassy clearing shown above —
a marvellous picnic spot. Carry on
through the clearing, walking
briefly through a few more trees,
to cross a dry stream bed. Follow
the TARGET MARKS up to a path
junction in the open, boulder-
strewn area of **Okrešelj**
(**1h04min**). You are now in the
centre of an amphitheatre of high,
craggy peaks — a scene of real
drama. Of the two paths that
continue up, the right-hand one is
the easiest to follow, as it makes
for Savinjško Sedlo on the
Austrian border. Sit awhile and
watch the progress of
mountaineers and climbers
heading for the tops.
Then head back down, past the

131

dom, to the path junction one minute beyond **Izvir Savinje** and take the path signposted, 'LOG. DOLINA, PASTIRSKA POT'. *(Note: this path is prone to landslides. Do not proceed if you cannot cross the scree slope and gullies easily; return to the main path and descend by the outward route.)* The path traverses the hillside, very quickly crossing a scree slope with a cable handrail. After another eight minutes you reach a wide gully where the path has slipped away. You will need to scramble up into the trees to cross it, aiming for wooden steps on the far side. Climb these and then descend steeply, following TARGET MARKS, back to the main path. After negotiating another gully, you begin the descent. The path zigzags down through beautiful beech woods, to eventually reach the CAR PARK (**2h09min**).

The descent through beech woods on the Pastirska Pot (Dairyman's Path)

41 PODOLŠEVA (SV. DUH) • POTOČKA ZIJAVKA • GOVCA • PODOLŠEVA (SV. DUH)

See also photo page 34, top right
Distance/time: 10km/6.3mi; 4h44min
Grade: strenuous, with a total ascent of approximately 800m/2625ft and a *very* steep descent from the ridge. Good mountain paths throughout
Equipment: see page 38; walking boots, walking sticks, torch
How to get there: 🚍 See Car tour 6, page 33. Park off the road near Sv. Duh in Podolševa.
Nearest accommodation: Logarska Dolina, Celje
Short walk: Sv. Duh — Potočka Zijavka — Sv. Duh. 4km/2.5mi; 1h50min. Moderate, with an ascent of 443m/1453ft. Equipment and access as main walk. Follow the main walk to Potočka Zijavka, then retrace your steps.

This walk is one of our favourites. Here, Slovenia seems timeless, rural life continuing much as it has done for centuries. We step in and out of Austria, explore a magnificent cave, and enjoy a 360-degree panorama from the high ridge.

Begin at the church **Sv. Duh** in Podolševa. Follow the unsurfaced road northeast downhill for six minutes, then fork left up a track to **Rogar**, an attractive farm. There is a sign, 'POTOČKA ZIJAVKA 1HR' just before the 7.5km distance marker. Walk up to the farm and look for an arrow and TARGET MARKS that direct you to a covered passageway between the buildings. Then take the track that climbs above and to the left of the farmhouse. Fork right just past the house and climb steeply up into the forest (well waymarked). The track crosses a small stream, where you turn left. Then follow the TARGET MARKS directing you up a path that climbs steeply to a gravel forestry track. Cross it and keep climbing for another 16 minutes, to a sign warning that you have reached the STATE BOUNDARY ('Pozor! Državna Menja'; **39min**). Follow the boundary for 10 minutes, to a junction. If you turn left for a few paces you will be in Austria! But we turn right, to **Potočka Zijavka (1h02min)**. Use your torch to explore this cave and *take care* — it can be very slippery. From the grassy ledge in front of the entrance there are spectacular views to the Kamniško-Savinjske

Alps, the valleys of Logarska Dolina and Matkov Kot and back down to Sv. Duh. *(The Short walk returns from here).*
The path now climbs a short, but steep, rocky gully to the right of the cave. A 20m length of secured cable will give you confidence and there are many good footholds (this is the hardest part of the walk). The path continues zig-zagging up the gully, to eventually leave it by a tall pointed rock. You then traverse across the slope under some amazing cliffs, to a junction. (We now *leave* the way-marked path shown on Slovenian maps and signposted 'Najvisji Vrh Olševe', because it soon leads to a secured, but potentially dangerous scramble down a loose rocky slope.) Turn *left* here; after a short distance 'OBEL KAMEN', your next objective, is painted on a rock. Continue climbing on the clear path to reach the end of the ridge, **Obel Kamen (1h29min)**, just on the BORDER BETWEEN SLOVENIA AND AUSTRIA. From the large wooden cross that marks the summit you can enjoy extensive views of Austria, but more breathtaking are the spectacular Kamniško-Savinjske Alps. Do not forget to sign the book!

From here, walk eastwards on a path that either follows the *RIDGE CREST AND BORDER* or is just to the right of it. After six minutes you reach another little top where the border leaves the ridge and heads off to the north. In another nine minutes, on a grassy top looking out over some rock towers, you come to a steep descent. The descent is not exposed, but you *will* need to use your hands and be surefooted here. Walk between the rock towers to a path (the way-marked route on the Slovenian maps) a few metres before regaining the crest. Continue along the ridge to reach **Govca** (**2h03min**), where you can perform another book-signing ceremony.

The route continues by following the ridge for a short way before leaving it and descending to the right. The path, still waymarked, descends and traverses to reach the crest again at a little grassy COL (**2h18min**). Keep to the ridge, climbing a little at first. It is quite different in character now, being much broader. Follow the faint path to a signpost (**2h34min**) and turn right towards SOLČAVA on a descending traverse towards a *TARGET-MARKED BOULDER*. (There's a sign on a tree nearby, 'OŠOVNIK OB CESTI'.) From here the narrow, knee-crunching path descends steeply through the forest. Rest your aching legs at one of the little rocky viewpoints along the way. Eventually the path becomes a track, and five minutes later you reach the road opposite a *FARM* (**3h54min**).

Turn right along the unsurfaced road, passing the left turn down to Solčava. Even the best walks have a sting in their tail — it is now uphill all the way back to **Sv. Duh** in **Podolševa** (**4h44min**)!

On the Austrian border just east of Obel Kamen, looking towards Govca